SpeedPro Series

HOW TO PLAN
& BUILD A
FAST
ROAD CAR

Contents

SPEEDPRO SERIES

Introduction & general principles

What is performance? The word 'performance' means different things to different people, but for the purposes of this book performance has four aspects -

Acceleration
Deceleration (braking)
Straightline top speed
Cornering speed

Each aspect of performance can be defined in a way that is useful when modifying a car. The definition can help you decide what tuning options to pursue.

Acceleration = engine torque to vehicle weight ratio. Increasing torque or reducing weight (or both), assuming a reasonable level of grip, will improve the acceleration of the vehicle.

Deceleration = braking torque (from brakes) to vehicle weight ratio, assuming a reasonable level of grip. Increasing either braking torque or reducing weight (or both) will improve the deceleration of the vehicle, *e.g.*, will shorten stopping distances.

Straightline top speed = ratio of engine horsepower (brake horsepower) to the coefficient of drag of the vehicle. Strictly speaking, rolling friction and other factors should also be taken into consideration, but can largely be ignored because, at speeds over 100mph, the drag is the limiting factor. Improving horsepower or reducing drag (or both) will raise the straightline top speed. Depending on the vehicle itself, and the desired top speed, it can be more beneficial to reduce drag than to increase horsepower.

Cornering speed = grip to weight ratio. Increasing grip or reducing weight (or both) will increase cornering speeds but, to a large extent, it's also important how the grip is used - a function of suspension.

Looking at each of the four aspects of performance, and what it takes to improve or raise performance, it can be seen that -

1. Reducing vehicle weight improves three aspects of performance.
2. Increasing grip improves one aspect of performance but can have a benefit on two others within certain parameters.
3. Increasing engine power and torque improves two aspects of performance.
4. Reducing coefficient of drag improves one aspect of performance.

Of course, this is only a guide and there are always exceptions, particularly where an existing aspect of performance is well below what might be considered average. For example, if a vehicle has particularly narrow wheels and tyres, the limiting factor in its acceleration, deceleration, and cornering performance might be its lack of grip. Therefore, although considerably wider wheels and tyres might well raise the weight of the vehicle - thereby reducing its torque to weight ratio - this disadvantage would be outweighed by the benefits yielded by the improvements in grip. So, although these listed aspects of performance have their limitations, within reason they will point you in the right direction.

PLANNING

When you are planning modifications to your vehicle, you need to decide what aspects of performance are most important to you and how much you have to spend (your budget). It's useful to consider the phrase "chasing a little horsepower with a lot of money". The first improvements you make will come quite cheaply but, at some point, further improvements become expensive. In racing, where the cars in any given class conform to a certain set of regulations, it's worth the extra expense if the difference is between winning and finishing. On the road this is not true because that money might well be better spent on buying a car with better performance rather than modifying the car you already have.

On the subject of how much it's all going to cost, it's only really in the areas of acceleration and straightline top speed that you can put a price on the benefit gained. For instance, you could say that an engine modification that produced a gain of 5bhp (for example fitting a K&N performance air filter) and costing approximately £50 (a bargain) works out at £10 per bhp. In practice, it's less easy to say how much quicker the car will go with that 5bhp.

Bear in mind, though, that sometimes tuning is not so straightforward and that extra 5bhp might have a hidden cost in that it takes your total engine output over the design limit of the clutch. What this means is that you might need to buy an uprated clutch before, or when, it breaks. In addition, at some point you might even have an engine that is so powerful that it breaks driveshafts or

Whether you want to fit an ITG cold air box to your Citroen Saxo to increase engine power ... (Courtesy - ITG)

halfshafts and so on.

However, it is not just power that makes acceleration and straightline top speed, but weight savings and aerodynamic improvements as well. These can also greatly improve the cornering speed of the car which, in my opinion, will produce the greatest satisfaction. With a weight saving you can cost every kg saved. For instance, a switch to alloy brake calipers might yield a saving of around 3-4kg (depending on original caliper size) at a cost of around £220. This works out at around £64/kg. If you compare this to other weight savings you will see whether or not it is money well spent. However, there are hidden factors - in this example a hidden benefit - the brake calipers are unsprung weight (see Chapter 13 - Suspension), and an unsprung weight saving produces a higher than normal increase in handling and ride benefits compared to

other weight savings. Further, the new calipers might also increase braking torque (shorter stopping distances).

Having worked out costs per unit of bhp and weight you may want to compare one type of improvement against another. To this end you can consider that 5kg equates to about 1bhp.

Finally, never lose sight of the fact that any weight saving yields benefits in three areas of performance, and when that weight saving is in unsprung weight, or anything that rotates at speed, the gain is even more beneficial. The smart money is always on weight saving, just look at the Lotus Elise!

ACKNOWLEDGEMENTS
Michael Ainsworth of Monroe Europe (UK) Ltd. Alloy Wheels International. Autocar Electrical Ltd. David Anton of APT. James Bailey of Goodyear Dunlop Tyres UK Ltd. Peter Baldwin.

Norman Barker of AP Racing. Geoff Barnes of AP Lockheed. BARS. Hugh Beeching of Flowtech Racing. Joe Bennett of AP Racing. Andrew D Burns of Kent Cams. Burton Power. Krystyna Chustecka of FFD Ricardo Ltd. Nigel Corry of Jamex. George Daniels of Autocar Electrical Ltd. Stephen Dodd of Safety Devices. Edelbrock. David Elderfield of Rally Design. Brian Ellis. Stuart Evans. Stephen Fell of Trans Auto Sport (UK). Goodyear. Rod Grainger, Alec Grant, and Kevin Quinn at Veloce. Christine Gregory - webmaster for TWM Induction. Jim Gurieff of Whiteline Automotive. Pete Hargrave of Yokohama H.P.T. Ltd. Ryan Herman of Wings West Inc. Holley. Richard Hughes (for donating his old PC). Peter Huxley of Fuel System Enterprises. Alan Jones of Jetex Exhausts Ltd. Peter Jones of Jondel Race Engines. Kenlowe Ltd. Andy King of ZF Great Britain Ltd. John Kirby of HKS Co Ltd. Simon A Lee of Janspeed. Jim Lodding of Unorthodox Racing Inc. Jim Losee of Edelbrock. Art Markus (motoring writer). Richard Marshall of Vegantune. Peter May. Monica Michelini of Brembo. Peter Mukherjee of Pentagon Auto-tint. Dave Musson of Speedograph Richfield Ltd. MWS Ltd. NGK. Andy Noble of Caterham Cars. Michael O'Connor. Tony Phillips of Kenlowe. Rob Potter of Think Automotive Ltd. Michael Quaife of RT Quaife Engineering Ltd. Bob Ritzman of B & M Racing and Performance Products. Keith Robertson of Fluidyne. Dave Robinson (graphic designer). Randy Robles of Focus Sport. Alan Rock of Stack. Ian Sandford of Superchips Ltd. Jon Savage of Cambridge Motorsport. Joni Schakel of Accessible Technologies, Inc (ProCharger). Ellwood Von Seibold of Spax. Serck Marston. Isobel Stapleton (my wife). TWM Induction. David Vizard. Ron Webb of GGB (Engineering Services) Ltd. Katja Weber of Eibach. Janet Wilkinson of the SMMT. Phil Woodcock of AP Lockheed. Suzanne Zelic of Eibach.

... or develop the handing of your car, this book will help you, along with providing information on every aspect of fast road car tuning. (Courtesy - Whiteline Automotive)

Using this book & essential information

USING THIS BOOK

Throughout this book the text assumes that you, or your contractor, will have a workshop manual specific to your car for complete detail on dismantling, reassembly, adjustment procedure, clearances, torque figures, etc.

You'll find it helpful to read the whole book before you start work or give instructions to your contractor. This is because a modification or change in specification in one area may cause the need for changes in other areas. Get the whole picture so that you can finalize specification and component requirements as far as is possible before any work begins.

For those wishing for more information on specific aspects of modification for high-performance there is a whole series of Veloce SpeedPro books (see page 5).

ESSENTIAL INFORMATION

This book contains information on practical procedures; however, this information is intended only for those with the qualifications, experience, tools and facilities to carry out the work in safety and with appropriately high levels of skill. Whenever working on a car or component, remember that your personal safety must **ALWAYS** be your **FIRST** consideration. **The publisher, author, editors and retailer of this book cannot accept any responsibility for personal injury or mechanical damage which results from using this book, even if caused by errors or omissions in the information given. If this disclaimer is unacceptable to you, please return the pristine book to your retailer who will refund the purchase price.**

In the text of this book **"Warning!"** means that a procedure could cause personal injury and **"Caution!"** that there is danger of mechanical damage if appropriate care is not taken. However, be aware that we cannot foresee every possibility of danger in every circumstance.

Please note that changing component specification by modification is likely to void warranties and also to absolve manufacturers of any responsibility in the event of component failure and the consequences of such failure.

Increasing the engine's power will place additional stress on engine components and on the car's complete driveline: this may reduce service life and increase the frequency of breakdown. An increase in engine power, and therefore the vehicle's performance, will mean that your vehicle's braking and suspension systems will need to be kept in perfect condition and uprated as appropriate. It is also usually necessary to inform the vehicle's insurers of any changes to the vehicle's specification.

The importance of cleaning a component thoroughly before working on it cannot be overstressed. Always keep your working area and tools as clean as possible. Whatever specialist cleaning fluid or other chemicals you use, be sure to follow - completely - the manufacturer's instructions and if you are using flammable liquids to clean parts, take every precaution necessary to protect your body and to avoid all risk of fire.

Chapter 1

Engine

On initial consideration, modifications to an engine will change only two, or perhaps three, aspects of performance - more power to raise straightline top speed and more torque to improve acceleration. It may be, however, that an increase in power will also raise cornering speeds (more so when engine modifications are carried out in conjunction with other modifications that improve cornering speed).

Going beyond the aforementioned performance gains, it can be the case that engine modifications will produce a reduction in weight - reducing weight and, at the same time, increasing power represents the ultimate in value for money in that all four aspects of performance are improved to some extent. One such modification would be replacing a standard cast iron cylinder head with a high performance, aluminium alloy one. Although this type of modification is often one of the most expensive, it might be one worth saving for. At the other end of

This alloy engine block is a replacement for the standard cast iron item and represents a very useful weight saving - but it will be expensive.

the spectrum would be a modification that dramatically increases power and torque, but puts considerable weight into the car, and where you least want it - at the front end, high up. A modification that falls into this category is turbocharging a previously normally aspirated engine.

Because the diverse scenarios outlined above can, and do, arise, you need to carefully consider and plan

the work you intend doing to your engine. Before that, though, you need a basic understanding of the principles of how the engine works in order to know whether a tuning modification will produce power or torque (or both), and whether it will be at a useful point in the rev range. The term 'engine' usually refers to the four stroke (Otto) internal combustion engine, although diesel engines (compression ignition) can also be tuned, as can rotary (Wankel) engines. For all these engine types the basic principle does not change, only the method employed to get the extra power.

In the most basic terms, an engine sucks in air to which fuel is added and this mixture is then burnt. The waste products of the burning (combustion) are pumped out as exhaust gases. The actual power produced by an engine is a function of the force with which the burning and expanding mixture of fuel and air acts upon the piston (or rotor for rotary engines) which then moves

The Vegan Tune alloy twin cam head for the Ford Kent engine fitted in a Caterham 7. (Courtesy - Vegan Tune Ltd)

In this cutaway engine you can see how the valves (on both cylinders in view) sit in relation to the combustion chamber.

down (or around), eventually turning the wheels on the road.

To get more power from an engine of the types we are considering, a greater force needs to be produced and that generally means bigger explosions or explosions made more frequently (or both). Both require more fuel and air being available to be burnt. Here there is a choice for tuning purposes - a bigger engine, or more efficient use of the existing engine. Apart from fitting a bigger engine, an existing engine can have its capacity increased, for example, by boring and stroking (more of this later). Making more efficient use of an existing engine is more involved, and requires some further basic explanation.

As the engine sucks air mixed with fuel into its combustion chambers, the mixture is prevented from escaping

before it is burned by a system of valves. Usually there will be one or two valves to let the air/fuel mixture in and the same number (usually) to prevent it getting out. These are the inlet and exhaust (outlet) valves. The opening and closing of the valves is controlled by one or more camshafts driven from the crankshaft by a toothed belt, chain or gears. The camshaft, or camshafts, act either directly or indirectly (via pushrods and rockers) to open and close the valves. To get more fuel/air mixture into the engine in order to produce more power, several things need to be considered: firstly, the size and shape of the route(s) through the cylinder head (the ports) to the valves and then to the combustion chamber; secondly, the shape of the combustion chamber, including the area around the valves; thirdly, the size, and to a

lesser extent the shape, of the valves; fourthly, the speed, extent, and length of time of valve opening. These factors are all controlled by the camshaft and are known as 'duration' and 'lift' (speed of opening does not have a specific name).

In deciding what to change, always remember the difference between engine torque and engine horsepower. Increases in engine torque improve vehicle acceleration, whereas increases in horsepower will improve the vehicle's top speed. You must consider which is more important to you, and make your choices accordingly, because some engine modifications will increase horsepower more than torque (even reduce torque at certain points in the rev range). Other engine tuning modifications will increase both torque and bhp. One

Having your cake and eating it - a bigger engine, tuned and with forced induction.

well-known and respected engine tuning company expressed the dilemma as, "horsepower sells engines, but torque wins races". The quote stands good in a road car context because torque makes for good acceleration and drivability. A peaky engine with lots of horsepower, but little torque, would be tiresome to drive on the road, other than on very long and fast straights.

Having gone through the very basics of what engine tuning is about, this brief explanation will be referred to, and amplified by specific examples, throughout this chapter, and others.

Coupled to our basic engine tuning theory, it is necessary to understand what units of measurement are used in respect of engine power outputs, and how to convert from one unit of measurement to another for purposes of comparison.

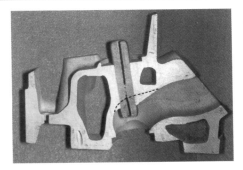

A section of a Rover V8 cylinder head reveals that the port is smaller in section around the valve guide (which is protruding). The faint pencil line indicates where the engine tuner would remove metal to improve gas flow.

In the early days of motoring the car was known as the 'horseless carriage' and its power compared to that of the horse; the term 'horsepower' was coined, and has largely stuck ever since. However, there are American, British (or imperial), and metric units of horsepower, as well as other commonly used units of power measurement. Metric horsepower is usually abbreviated as PS, which is an abbreviation for Pferdestarke (the German word for horsepower). A single unit of horsepower (SAE) is equal to 1.0139 PS, 745.70 Watts or 0.7457 kilo Watts (kW).

As far as torque is concerned, to convert from Nm to lb/in multiply by 8.851 and for lb/in to Nm multiply by 0.113 (remembering to convert the inches to feet to get the final answer when going from Nm to lb/ft).

Time to start to plan what is to be done to the engine. The following list suggests an order of priority for making the key decisions -

1. Is torque or horsepower to be the

This cutaway drawing of the Chevrolet Northstar V8 engine reveals all of the working components of an engine. (Courtesy - Chevrolet)

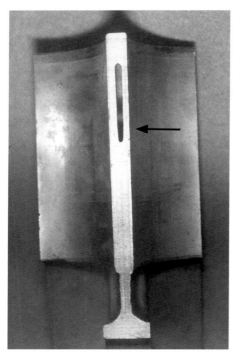

A section between a pair of cylinders shows us that what you might assume is a thick block wall actually gets very thin at its top, near the water jacket.

A closer look at the valves, 2 inlet and 2 exhaust on this engine. The valves are operated by a pair of camshafts via cam followers or 'buckets'.

dominant gain?
2. Amount of gain sought?
3. Rev limit of engine (if tuning will raise above standard)?
4. Amount of money available?

BORING & STROKING

As mentioned earlier in the chapter, one way to increase the capacity of an engine is by boring the cylinders to a larger diameter and/or stroking. The 'bore' of the engine is the diameter of the cylinder and corresponding pistons. The 'stroke' is the distance the piston travels on each stroke (not the length of the cylinder).

As with units of power, there is more than one common measure. Generally, the engine size will be given in cubic centimetres (cc) calculated by multiplying the bore by the stroke. In the USA, it's usual to measure capacity using cubic inches. For instance, if you convert 7 litres (7.013 to be exact) to inches you get 428cu in. By comparison, the Buick 215 cubic inch engine sounds small but is, in reality, 3.523 litres (3523cc).

The limitation on boring the cylinders to a larger diameter, sometimes known as 'overboring', is dependent on the engine block casting, the thickness of the cylinder walls, and piston availability. So, for example, although a 1300cc engine can be bored out to 1400cc, it will never be bored out to 2000cc. However, any increase in capacity is useful and, if an engine is worn and needs a rebore, it's worth considering boring to a near maximum size rather than simply having it bored to the next oversize. Overboring can be a very cost effective way to get more power out of an engine (especially a tired one), though

once the engine is bored out to its maximum size, no further rebore will be possible and the engine block becomes scrap unless it is possible to fit new cylinder sleeves, something not possible on most if engines. Something to give consideration to at this time are the pistons and compression ratio, which are discussed later in the chapter.

'Stroking' an engine is when the crankshaft stroke is lengthened, which increases the swept volume of the cylinders by using more of their length. Sometimes an engine can be stroked by replacing the crank with one from a larger capacity engine from the same family, though it might be easier to use the whole engine if it is available. In other instances, small increases in stroke can be achieved by a machine shop grinding the crank differently. The largest changes in stroke will come from having a special crankshaft made, which will be quite expensive, and not necessarily feasible on all types of engine.

When boring and stroking are combined, anything from a reasonable to a hefty increase in engine capacity can be achieved, which can produce a useful increase in power over the standard engine (in rough proportion to the size of the increase in capacity). Always consider that it might well be

Looking up the bore from the crankcase - the use of a long throw crank can necessitate removal of metal on anything that might get in the way of the longer throw.

simpler and cheaper to use a bigger engine in the first place.

Boring and stroking are subject to limitations imposed by the cylinder head(s). Any head can be improved, more of which later, to improve the speed and/or volume of the fuel/air mixture flowing through it. However, at some point an absolute maximum of gasflow will be reached. This absolute maximum will vary from head to head, but it's a point worth checking with an engine specialist familiar with the engine you are planning to tune before commencing the building of a super-size bored and stroked engine. The reason for this caution is that the engine may fail to realise its full potential in relation to its capacity because of the limitations of the head(s).

CRANKSHAFT MODIFICATIONS

There are a variety of modifications

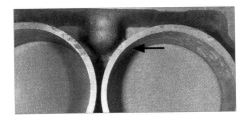

This section of a cylinder wall reveals a small crack - a result of boring to the point where wall strength is compromised.

When a crank breaks it can wreck the rest of the engine, so always get it crack tested. This one failed due to over-revving from a missed gear change.

that can be made to the crankshaft. However, the first thing to have done to any crank is crack testing. (**Caution!** - only if the crank is OK is it worth proceeding with other work.) If the crank does have cracks, it is best scrapped.

The two most common operations performed on cranks are balancing and hardening; these two operations are performed by a specialist machine shop to both strengthen the crank and increase its resistance to fatigue. The cost is reasonable in respect to many other operations and is money well spent. Other work done to the crank is done to reduce fatigue and improve the oil supply to the crank bearings, but is much less likely to be necessary for road use unless very high rpm usage is envisaged. Finally, if the crank breaks it is likely to trash the rest of the engine, including the block and head.

COMPRESSION RATIO INCREASES

The compression ratio (CR) is expressed as a ratio of one. For instance, 9.5 to one, 9.5 to 1, or 9.5:1. What this means in practical terms is that 9.5 units of space occupied by the air/fuel mixture drawn into the engine (piston at bottom of cylinder) are compressed to just one unit when the piston is at the top of the cylinder. The higher the compression ratio, the more the mixture is 'squeezed.' An increase in CR is something to be considered as part of the overall tuning process. A change in camshaft may dictate an increase in CR, whereas a change to forced induction, such as turbocharging, may dictate no change, or maybe even a reduction, in CR. Increases in CR should be carefully considered because an engine that has too high a CR will require a higher fuel octane rating if it is to run without self-destructing. Changes in CR can be

effected in several ways.

One way to increase the CR is by skimming the cylinder head or engine block, the latter to a lesser extent, in order to reduce the space the fuel/air mixture will be compressed into in relation to the swept volume (bore x stroke) of the engine. Another way is to use high compression pistons which have a reduced dish in the piston crown (top), flat, or domed crowns.

The CR can be reduced by changing pistons to ones with a dish in the crown or larger dish in the crown, or increased combustion chamber size created by enlarging the chamber.

Caution! - Never use a CR that causes 'pinking'/'pinging' with the ignition timing set within the correct parameters.

CYLINDER HEAD MODIFICATIONS
Changes to the combustion chamber

The combustion chamber in the cylinder head is where it all happens. After the fuel/air mixture has travelled down the inlet ports and through an open valve, the valve is closed and the mixture is compressed by the rising piston until it is densely squeezed into the combustion chamber. On all engines the top of the piston,

Not all cylinder head work equates to the removal of vast amounts of metal, as can be seen by the suitable but very useful work done to this Renault 5 Turbo head.

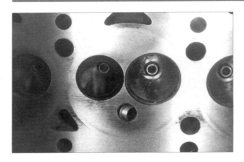

On some engines the combustion chamber is in the piston crown and the valves and cylinder head form a flat surface.

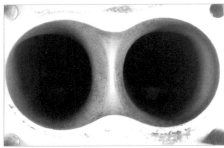

Looking down these ports you can just see the valve seat area.

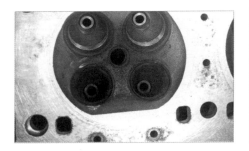

The marks (shiny area) by the bottom left hand valve (exhaust) were caused by a damaged, possibly bent or broken, valve contacting the cylinder head, which led to an expensive engine failure.

This cylinder head section illustrates how the valves form part of the combustion chamber. The centre punch marking was used to test for porosity of the casting.

the crown, also forms part of the combustion chamber. Next, the compressed fuel/air mixture is ignited by a spark delivered by the sparkplugs. Crucially, it is how the flame front created by the spark travels through the combustion chamber that dictates, to some extent, the amount of power produced. The combustion needs to be smooth and rapid. Further, because it is happening in very short periods of time, the distance the flame travels needs to be as short as possible. Once ignited, the fuel/air mixture rapidly expands and the resulting force pushes outwards in all directions but, of course, the only components yielding to the force are the pistons, which are forced down the cylinder bore.

Usually, modifications to the

combustion chamber centre around ensuring that the valves are not shrouded - that is, too close to the chamber walls such that the incoming fuel/air mixture is obstructed on the way in and, likewise, the exhaust gas on its way out. For some engines this is not a problem, or only becomes one when larger sized valves are fitted.

There is also a benefit in precisely equalising the volume of each combustion chamber. Very occasionally it is desirable to alter the shape of the combustion chamber more radically (by welding, for example) to add extra metal in certain places, but such work is not cheap. Most head work can be do-it-yourself, but only if you have a good reference work particular to the head

you are modifying, a good, proven example to copy, and generally know what you are doing. If you have any doubt, it is far better to know what you are looking for and then purchase accordingly.

Changes to valve sizes
I think it will be helpful, when considering increasing valve sizes, to think about what the valves are actually doing. Imagine yourself at home on a hot day, you decide to open a window to let some fresh air in - the window opens the room to the outside atmosphere. Returning to engine tuning, think of the valve in the cylinder head opening the cylinder head combustion chamber to the outside atmosphere and letting in the air and fuel mixture. Imagine yourself back at home again and, assuming your house's window frames have big and small windows, it is obvious that the bigger window will let more fresh air in. Well, it's just the same with engine valves - a bigger inlet valve will let more fuel and air in, and a bigger exhaust valve will let more exhaust gas out (all other things being equal). Given our basic principle that more fuel and air will provide greater combustion and therefore a greater push to drive the piston down the cylinder, and so on, bigger valves (in association with enlarged ports) will allow the engine to produce more power.

Porting
Because the size and shape of the ports control, to a large extent, the volume and speed of the fuel/air mixture flow to and from the combustion chambers, they have an important effect on performance tuning. Although you might think that increasing the port size would instantly produce more power, this is not always the case because the

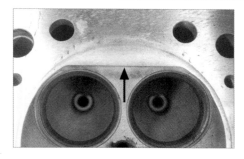

Too much compression, too low a fuel octane, or too much ignition advance are just three things which can cause the engine to detonate: the matt surface of this surface area shows the result in a mild form.

This Weslake design, 6 port head is a direct performance replacement for the 4 port item on the Ford V6 Cologne engine, and is one route to realising more power from the engine.

Supposedly superior to the four valve per combustion chamber head is the five valve per combustion chamber head. Whilst used on motorcycle engines as illustrated here it has been used on only a few car engines.

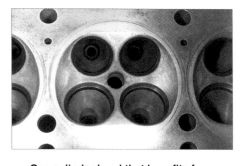

One cylinder head that benefits from porting more than an increase in valve size is the Ford BD series head, a chamber of which is shown here.

Typical port opening into combustion chamber.

The shiny area that can be seen on these ports are where metal has been removed to improve gas flow.

speed of the gas can drop dramatically and reduce the total volume of gasflow. However, just as ports can be too large they can also be too small, and an expert engine tuner will know what is best for your particular engine. The shape of the port is important because sharp turns can be detrimental to gasflow and, again, an expert engine tuner will know how to reshape the port to get the best result. Because porting is not only specialised, but specific to particular engines, it is beyond the scope of this book to cover it in detail.

CYLINDER HEAD SWAPS

For some engines, rather than spend

Four valve per combustion chamber heads are generally considered superior to two valve per combustion chamber heads but for fast road cars the difference is not so great.

When changing the camshaft you will also need to change the cam followers and possibly the springs as well, all of which makes buying a complete kit, such as the ones shown here, the best way to achieve value for money. (Courtesy - Kent Cams)

Getting the cam timing exactly right is not easily achieved on some engines, if possible at all, without an adjustable timing pulley such as these items from Kent cams. (Courtesy - Kent Cams)

a lot of money modifying the cylinder head, there is the alternative of buying an off-the-shelf high performance head. Quite often this cylinder head will have twice as many valves as the standard head, or it may be a twin overhead cam design replacing a single, non-overhead unit. The high performance head will most likely use a superior combustion chamber design with optimised porting, and so on.

Many popular engines have alternative cylinder heads available for them in the after market.

CAMSHAFT CHANGES

A change in camshaft is a well-trodden path to an increase in engine performance, but one that has certain drawbacks and limitations. A basic introduction to how the camshaft functions in an engine is necessary

For other engines, like the Rover A-series, the standard cylinder head can be replaced by a high performance item like this head from Jack Knight.

The top drawing shows what cam lift and duration (period) are; the lower is an illustration of valve timing showing period of overlap.

Cam Period

Flank

Cam Lift

Inlet Opens 40°

TDC *Overlap* 90°

Exhaust Closes 50°

50°
Inlet closes

BDC

40°
Exhaust Opens

Pistons come in all shapes and sizes. This one has a domed crown with valve reliefs. (Courtesy - Cambridge Motorsport)

Whereas this piston is dished with valve reliefs. (Courtesy - Cambridge Motorsport)

far the valve opens (valve lift off the valve seat), how long the valve stays open, and when the inlet valves are open in relation to the exhaust valves. It is also possible to vary the timing of the opening and closing of the valves in relation to the movement of the pistons in the cylinders and this is known as 'camshaft timing'. In practice, cam timing is not so much changed to gain power but rather set to occur at precisely the right times to ensure no power is lost. With many after market high performance cams it is only possible to get the cam timing exactly right if adjustable cam timing pulleys/sprockets are used, although, if no suitable pulley is available, it's possible to use special offset Woodruff keys. Having had first hand experience of an engine with a mistimed high performance cam, I can say that an error of as little as 10 degrees can result in a loss of approximately 20 horsepower.

As far as cam selection goes, on the face of it, and in one sense this is true, the ideal way to get more power out of an engine is to fit a cam that will open the valves very quickly, a long way, and for a long time. However, returning to the 360 degree cycle, it is apparent that the inlet valve can only usefully remain open when the piston is going down and the cylinder drawing in the fuel/air mixture. This is 180 degrees. The remaining 180 degrees is required for the piston to go up the cylinder and compress the fuel/air mixture. For the next 360 degrees the inlet valve must remain closed while the combustion gasses push the piston down the cylinder, and remain closed when the piston comes up the cylinder to push out the exhaust gas via the exhaust valve. At this point there appears to be a problem because the inlet valve is open for 180 degrees but cannot remain open for more

before considering the tuning options.

Either directly or indirectly the camshaft controls the opening and closing of the valves. The actual size and profile of the lobes of the camshaft controls how quickly the valve opens, how far it opens, and how long it stays open. The valve springs actually close the valve but cannot close it any quicker than the cam will allow.

If you consider that a single revolution of the engine will consist of 360 degrees, it's possible to express

the length of time the valve is open in degrees and this is how the cam duration is measured. In addition, there is a time during the cycle of the engine that both inlet and exhaust valves are open together, this is known as 'valve overlap'. The relation between the cam lobes controlling the inlet valves and those controlling the exhaust valves is also a factor in the overall specification of the camshaft. To quickly summarise, the camshaft(s) control: speed of valve opening, how

than a quarter of the time the piston is moving. The problem is solved by rotating the camshaft(s) at half the engine speed, and this is achieved by the camshaft pulley/sprocket being half the diameter of the crankshaft pulley/sprocket.

VALVE GEAR MODIFICATIONS - ROCKER GEAR

For those engines where the valves are opened via rockers (or pushrods and rockers) there are useful changes that can be made to gain power and/or increase component life. Such rockers will either be of a higher ratio than the standard item (high lift rockers) and thereby increase lift at the valve independent of any camshaft change, or be of different construction and contact pad size to prevent premature failure in a performance application. High performance rockers are usually quite expensive, but they can represent good tuning value for money in relation to the increase in power they produce.

PISTONS

The piston is central to the amount of power produced in the engine because it does more than one job; it provides suction to draw in the fuel/air mixture, compresses it, is acted against during combustion, and then pushes out the exhaust gas. The piston is subject to high loadings and temperatures in the process.

A change in piston might be required for a variety of reasons. The most common is that the standard piston is not strong enough to withstand the loadings imposed by a power tuned engine and will most likely fail, particularly at high rpm. The difference, other than cost, is that standard pistons are made by casting the molten metal while performance pistons are forged by a stamping

process with semi-molten metal. The forged pistons are stronger.

High performance pistons will be lighter than standard pistons, though, in some instances, it's possible to lighten the standard ones. Piston weight is important because the greater the weight, the greater the energy absorbed in accelerating and decelerating the piston on each stroke, with three out of every four strokes producing no power.

Changes in engine compression may require a change in piston and changes in bore diameter will. When choosing pistons, balance cost against desirability. Finally, if you are turbo or supercharging what was previously a normally aspirated engine, you'll probably need completely different pistons from the standard ones - be guided by the turbo/supercharger manufacturer.

CON-RODS

The term con-rods is a shortened version of the name connecting rods and each rod connects a piston to the

crankshaft (on the crankshaft throw). The small end of the con rod is fitted to the piston by a large pin – more like a thick walled section of tube than a pin, while the large or better known big end of the con rod is joined to the crankshaft by means of being made in a section known as the cap which bolts to the main con rod body. For any engine where power and particularly rpm, has been increased some consideration needs to be given to the con rod. The con rod and not least the con rod bolts are, like the piston, subject to enormous loadings and can fail. A rod can bend or totally fail in tension, while, if the rod bolts themselves work loose or fail, complete failure of the rod ensues. Upgrades to the con-rods need not be expensive and the rods can be crack tested before being balanced and surface treated such as lead shot blasted or polished – alternative ways of relieving stresses that could contribute to failure. Not least replacement of the standard rod bolts by race quality rod bolts such as those from ARP is money well spent.

A nice touch if you can afford it is a decent set of steel con-rods. (Courtesy - Cambridge Motorsport)

Front wheel drive engine swaps can work with the right combination like a 2000cc engine from another Vauxhall model transplanted into the Corsa as shown here.

ENGINE SWAPS

When it comes to engine swaps, a front engined, rear wheel drive car has the greatest potential. Front engined, front wheel drive cars are often limited to a larger engine from the same engine family/manufacturer and, even then, things are not easy because of the way the gearbox is usually bolted directly to the crankcase.

In some cases, however, the engine swap is not all it might at first seem, because it is based on the original engine or engine block. An example of this type of conversion is the Vegantune VTA engine. This

engine is based on Ford's Kent engine block; the most obvious difference lies with the cylinder head which is an alloy twin cam unit. The engine can be built to various road or full race specifications in 1600 or 1700cc sizes. Vegantune claim 100bhp at 4000rpm going on to a peak of 170bhp at 7000rpm.

If you are going to do an engine swap, make sure your decision is based on the clean sheet of paper rule. In other words, decide what engine you actually want rather than decide to use an engine you just happen to have kicking around. Because your

engine swap is likely to involve fitting a larger and more powerful engine, be wary of the ills of a large weight gain at the front of the car, which will create difficult-to-solve handling problems.

The tuneability of the replacement engine is an important consideration because there is not a lot of point having a 3.5 litre V8 in the engine bay if a similar car to yours blows you into the weeds with a tuned 2 litre engine that was a lot less hassle to fit (it came with the car), and probably cost less money to sort. Of course, depending on the car you have, the biggest limitation may well be engine

A decent rocker or cam cover, such as the pair shown here for a Ford Essex V6 from Burton Power, make even a standard engine look businesslike. (Courtesy - Burton Power)

Engine swaps can entail swapping to a larger size, such as from 1.4 K series to 1.8K series.

Alternatively, the engine swap can be to a different make and larger size, such as this Fiat twin cam installed in a Ford.

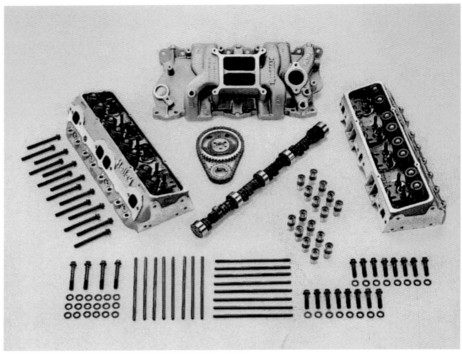

For some popular engines, complete tuning kits are available which include head(s), cam(s) and manifold(s) such as this offering from Holley. (Courtesy - Holley)

bay space and this is why alloy V6 and V8 engines, which are relatively short (though wider), are popular substitutes for cast iron four cylinder units.

With any engine swap you can run into problems with the siting of ancillaries and a variety of engine bay components. One particular problem is that of the oil filter. There are a range of takeoff plates that can be used to replace the existing filter head and filter. The takeoff plate, once fitted, will need to be piped to a remote filter head and, quite possibly, via an oil cooler. See Chapter 8 - Engine

lubrication & oil cooling, for further details.

ENGINE MOUNTINGS

Whatever engine you have fitted in your vehicle, and in particular if it is an unusual engine swap, you can run into problems with engine mountings. One company who specialise in compliance technology (rubbers and mountings) is Vibra Technics. They have a range of suitable high performance engine and transmission mountings for all kinds of vehicles.

Chapter 2
Engine management & ignition systems

INTRODUCTION

Improvements to the engine management or ignition system may also improve engine torque and horsepower, thereby affecting two aspects of performance - acceleration and straightline top speed. However, because the improvements may also include an improved throttle response and the elimination of flat spots, cornering speeds may improve also (not to mention cornering speeds in very fast bends by virtue of having more power). Cold starting will also improve, although this is not an aspect of performance.

Modifications to the engine management system (CPU controlled systems only) will involve having the main chip changed or reprogrammed - this will be most beneficial to cars which have forced induction systems added. More recently it has become possible to have the chip tailored to take into account changes to the engine induction and exhaust systems

with attendant benefits (more of which later).

Modifications to the ignition system of your vehicle may not, by themselves, change any aspect of the vehicle's performance. However, if the ignition system becomes inadequate (because of high performance tuning) for the requirements of the engine, it can prevent the engine realising its true potential - not to mention making it a swine to start. Ultimately though, it is generally the case that if your car's engine has been tuned for more power it will be more demanding in its ignition requirements.

SPARKPLUGS

Arguably the most important thing about the sparkplug in a modified engine is not so much what type or make it is, though those can matter, but rather the temperature range of the plug.

High performance engines need 'colder' (harder) plugs than standard

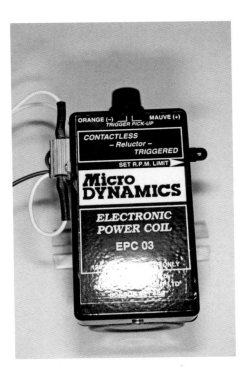

Matched coil and ignition system complete with rev limiter, as shown here in the Microdynamics Electronic Power Coil, ensures ignition system compatibility.

engines. If you are tuning an engine with a view to increasing its power output, you will need to consider changing plug grades, perhaps by one grade or sometimes more. When trying to determine the optimum heat range it's worth seeking advice from reputable engine tuners familiar with your car's engine type. Start with cold (hard) plugs and work down to softer ones to get it right and prevent damage being done at the selection stage. Note that plugs which are too hot (soft) for your engine can be a cause of pre-ignition knocking (pinking/pinging) during hard use of the engine. Also, they may cause the engine to run on after it has been switched off. **Caution!** - Prolonged use of plugs which are too hot, can damage the engine, most notably the piston crown, ultimately resulting in a terminal, and expensive, failure. Finally, you should note that the numbering sequences used by the plug manufacturers vary. For instance, Champion and NGK number in opposite directions in relation to the heat range, and some motor factors are ignorant of this.

HIGH TENSION (HT) LEADS (PLUG WIRES)

HT leads have some resistance to electrical current. Many original equipment HT leads are manufactured using carbon inpregnated string, which

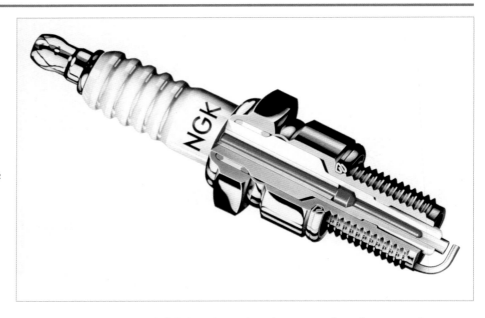

This cutaway of an NGK plug shows there is more to plugs than meets the eye. (Courtesy - NGK)

has a high resistance value (bad), and cease to function effectively after approximately 20,000 miles.

For high performance use, or just the best possible cold starting performance, there are better alternatives to carbon string-type leads, though some will require a change of coil and distributor cap to suit their push-fit connectors.

Good high performance HT leads are the silicone-insulated type, with wires wound around ferrite cores.

For the best results, always buy those with the lowest quoted resistance.

In the USA, Nology Engineering has produced an ignition lead with a difference: a built-in capacitor that allows spark energy from the coil to

High performance HT leads with a difference - Nology 'Hotwires'.

build up before being released to the sparkplug. This creates a spark of much shorter duration and greater intensity than is possible with more conventional high performance leads. The Nology leads differ from more conventional leads by having an earth (ground) strap which can be fastened to convenient earthing (grounding) points on the engine.

COIL

In the ignition system it is the coil that produces the high powered spark that, when delivered to the plugs, fires the fuel/air mixture. In most conventional ignition systems there will be one coil for the whole engine, as opposed to one small coil per cylinder as in many more modern systems. The coil has to produce sufficient power to ignite the fuel/air mixture under all circumstances so, while the standard coil may be fine for a production engine, it will usually be unsuitable for the same engine when it's tuned. It takes an amount

Changing from a standard coil to a high energy version such as the Lucas sports item shown here, will make a difference, not least to cold starting - sometimes a problem on highly-tuned engines.

of time for the coil voltage to recover after being discharged at the plug and, as the engine speed rises, the coil has less and less time to do this, until the point is reached when it can no longer produce an adequate spark. This state of affairs is often described as 'saturation' but, in actual fact, when the coil is inadequately charged, the correct description is that it is not reaching saturation. Terminology aside, the coil simply fails to deliver an adequate spark because it can't. If a saturation problem is not caused by inadequate dwell or by points bounce, the coil will need replacing with a higher rated unit.

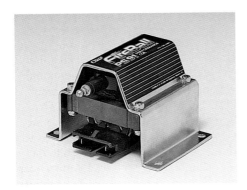

Not all coils are cylinders, as illustrated by this performance item from Crane Cams. (Courtesy - Crane Cams)

For most road tuned four and six cylinder engines it is not often that the engine rpm will be such that the standard coil will be inadequate. However, this is not the case on eight cylinder engines because the greater number of cylinders effectively doubles the work that the coil has to do. Looking at the problem another way, the coil has half as much time to produce the required voltage. Saturation can be overcome by fitting a suitable performance coil.

Sometimes a high performance coil will be known as a 'sports coil', as is the case with the Lucas brand. However, in other cases, the coil will be marketed as a 'high performance coil' or 'high energy coil', such as the Microdynamics item. Some coils need to be used in conjunction with a ballast resistor and this is a point worth checking before parting with your cash or destroying an electronic ignition system. However, if you use a coil that is not designed to be used with a ballast resistor all that happens is that the spark energy is reduced.

DISTRIBUTOR

In a conventional ignition system (i.e. no engine management chip), it is the distributor that ensures that the

spark from the coil is delivered at the sparkplug at the right time. Because the engine speed varies, the distributor has to cope with delivering the spark at the right time whatever the engine speed, and therein lies a problem - as the engine speed increases there is less time for everything to happen and, because of this, the spark needs to arrive slightly earlier in the combustion cycle. However, this only applies up to about the midpoint of the engine's speed range, typically about 3000rpm, or so. The distributor achieves this variable timing by having a rotating platform that is controlled by a mechanism of bob weights and springs. As the engine speed, and therefore distributor shaft speed, increases, the mechanism varies the position of the platform in relation to the distributor cap, thereby ensuring that the spark arrives earlier in the ignition cycle. Although this sounds quite complicated, it works well in practice (that is, until you start to powertune the engine).

Certain power tuning engine modifications, especially changes in camshaft and modified cylinder heads, change the ignition requirements such that at one or more particular points in the rev range more, or sometimes less, ignition advance is required; or the advance needs to be quicker.

Changes to a distributor's advance curve can only be effected by a change in the advance mechanism in the form of lighter/heavier bob weights and/or weaker/stronger springs. The easiest way to discover exactly what your engine's ignition advance requirements are is to run the engine on a dynamometer - for instance, a chassis dyno (rolling road) which can make a plot of the optimum ignition advance. An even easier way is to speak to a company with expertise in performance distributors, such

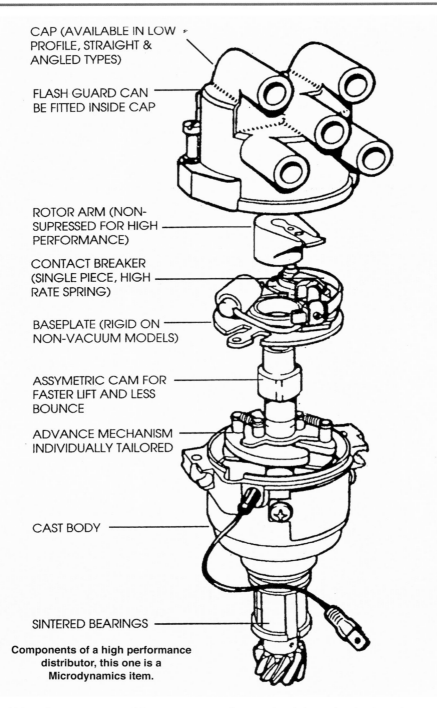

CAP (AVAILABLE IN LOW PROFILE, STRAIGHT & ANGLED TYPES)

FLASH GUARD CAN BE FITTED INSIDE CAP

ROTOR ARM (NON-SUPRESSED FOR HIGH PERFORMANCE)

CONTACT BREAKER (SINGLE PIECE, HIGH RATE SPRING)

BASEPLATE (RIGID ON NON-VACUUM MODELS)

ASSYMETRIC CAM FOR FASTER LIFT AND LESS BOUNCE

ADVANCE MECHANISM INDIVIDUALLY TAILORED

CAST BODY

SINTERED BEARINGS

Components of a high performance distributor, this one is a Microdynamics item.

CONVERSION TO ELECTRONIC IGNITION

If the engine in your car is fitted with a conventional contact breaker points ignition system, there are several benefits to converting to an electronic system which may be points triggered or wholly electronic. The main advantage, though, is not just a performance gain at high rpm, which is especially the case if the engine is modified such that it places greater demands on the coil, but a maintenance one as well. However, not having to regularly change ignition points when their performance tails away at the end of their life, at least ensures that the engine is realising its full power potential all the time. Before purchasing, though, think about what else you want, such as a rev limiter, shift light, and so on, because in the long run it can work out considerably cheaper to buy one system that does everything, rather than purchase separate components. The reverse can also be true, and, if you have a rev counter (or plan to purchase one) that has shift light functions, you won't need to pay extra for a shift light function on the ignition system.

ELECTRONIC IGNITION SYSTEMS
Contact breaker points triggered systems

It is possible to fit an electronic ignition system which, while providing a number of benefits, does in fact still retain a conventional contact breaker points system. Although, on the face of things, it might appear to make more sense to go all the way and have a fully electronic ignition system and have even more benefits, there are good reasons for not doing so. Perhaps the biggest advantage in using a points triggered ignition system is that it will often work out cheaper. More

as Aldon Automotive, and have it produce a suitable unit for you based on its experience of tuned engines. This unit can then be further tailored to the needs of the individual application, if necessary, after the rolling road session.

importantly, though, an electronically controlled points triggered system will not affect the distributor advance curve - an important consideration if you already run a distributor with a unique advance curve to suit the characteristics of the engine in your car. This type of electronic ignition is sometimes known as 'Transistor-Assisted Contacts coil ignition' (TAC). One product that fits this bill is the Microdynamics Electronic Power Coil (EPC01) which comprises: points triggered ignition system, adjustable rev limiter, and coil - all in one compact unit. This unit will not only improve the ignition system performance, but will also reduce points arcing - something which can be a problem when using a high output or sports coil. Note, however, that Microdynamics has other power coils for use with original equipment and other manufacturers' electronic systems, e.g. Lucas Inductor types.

Contact breakerless systems

If you intend to convert your engine's ignition system to a fully electronic system, you may need to have the advance curve of the distributor modified to suit - unless the distributor was specifically designed and built for electronic operation, or you have one of the few fully electronic systems that doesn't alter the advance curve. It's also important to check whether or not the system requires a ballasted coil. Having decided to fit a fully electronic system, you now have quite a wide choice of operation (three basic categories) and manufacturer. The advantages of a fully electronic system are the elimination of contact points bounce, arcing, and wear. However, unless you have a very high revving engine, running in the high 7000rpm region, the main benefit over electronic points triggered systems is the reduction of wear.

Crane Cams has a range of performance ignition systems; this one is used to replace unreliable original equipment units. (Courtesy - Crane Cams)

Lumenition has a wide range of performance ignition products; athis is a kit for converting points triggered distributors to an optical system. (Courtesy - Autocar Electrical Ltd)

Here you can see the Aldon Ignitor installed in a typical Lucas distributor.

Optical type systems

Perhaps the most well known fully electronic systems are the optically triggered kits from Lumenition in the UK, or Crane in the USA and UK. Both systems come with comprehensive fitting instructions, and the 'black box', that forms an integral part of the system, can be located on the pedalbox cover or inner wing, which will permit the wiring runs to be kept short and the unit well away from excessive heat, dampness or vibration, though the Lumenition is fully encapsulated for maximum protection against vibration and dampness. Specific to the Lumenition kit is what the company calls 'the classic mounting bracket', which locates under the coil bracket and allows mounting of the 'black box' without having to drill any holes in your car.

Magnetic type (Hall effect) systems

An alternative to the optical systems are the magnetic type systems. There are two manufacturers' products to choose from, and both have an advantage over optical systems in that they are wholly contained inside the distributor cap without an external 'black box'. One system is the Ignitor (available as the Aldon Ignitor in the UK), the other the Magnetronic from Lumenition. The systems are similar, and both replace contact breakers and condensers.

Variable reluctance/reluctor (inductor type) systems

Nowadays, the least common type of fully electronic system is the variable reluctance/reluctor, or inductor type. Usually, this type of system was purchased not so much as a conversion kit for an existing distributor, but as a distributor and accompanying 'black box', or sometimes as an ignition package to work with existing original equipment electronic distributors. If you have an original, or even after market, inductor ignition it can usually be improved upon by fitting the Microdynamics EPC03 Power Coil, which includes a rev limiter, or to a lesser extent by fitting a suitable sports coil on its own.

This is what the Lucas inductor factory fit electronic ignition looks like - it can be used with a combined high performance coil and rev-limiter unit from Lumenition.

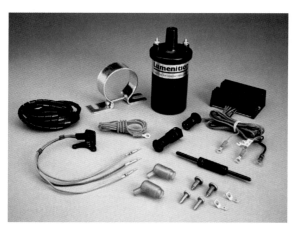

This Lumenition kit includes everything you need for performance ignition, including the coil. (Courtesy - Autocar Electrical Ltd)

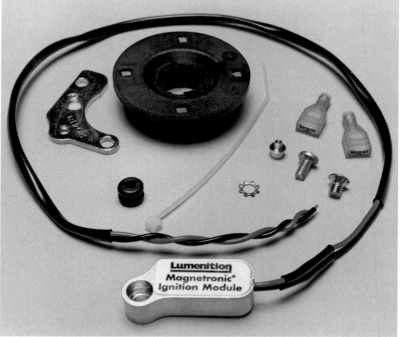

Magnetic (Hall effect) electronic ignition system from Lumenition that will fit inside any existing distributor. (Courtesy - Autocar Electrical Ltd)

REV LIMITERS

One benefit of having a well tuned and modified road engine is that the engine has a greater rpm potential than the standard engine. In fact, it may have so much potential that hanging on to one of the lower gears such as first or second, during a bout of hard acceleration can result in excessive rpm being used leading to a range of engine damage some of which can be terminal to the engine's life. You may get away with it once or twice, or possibly not at all. The damage is caused by the excessive rpm overloading components such as pistons, con-rods, or con rod bolts leading to complete failure or contact between the valves and pistons where the valve springs simply cannot get the valves out of the piston's way fast enough, likewise leading to complete failure. To prevent the problem of over-revving a rev limiter should be fitted.

Rev limiters usually take one of three forms: the type that cuts the ignition; the type that cuts the fuel supply; or the type that cuts the ignition and fuel supply. Some modern engines, with a comprehensive engine management system, will have a rev limiter incorporated into the system. Older engines may have a separate limiter and, if they don't, you'll need to purchase one as a component in its own right. If you intend to upgrade the ignition system, perhaps converting to an electronic system, it may be possible to purchase a system that has a rev limiting function built in.

ENGINE MANAGEMENT CHIP CHANGES

Chipping an engine to increase its performance seems like the simplest and cheapest way to get horsepower increases from your engine. However, not all engines can be chipped, and some will produce more power from a

Micro Dynamics produces this rev-limiter and others, some of which are part of ignition systems. (Courtesy - Autocar Electrical Ltd)

chip change than others.

If your car's engine doesn't have an electronic engine management system, there will be nothing to chip. Also, if the engine is normally aspirated (i.e. not turbocharged/supercharged), the power gains will usually be in the region of 10 per cent horsepower and 15 per cent torque, at least with Superchips brand chips anyway. If the engine is turbocharged/supercharged, and has a management system with a chip, then it can be chipped, but you have to understand what effect this has

A typical performance chip - this one from Superchips. (Courtesy - Superchips Ltd)

on the engine and drive train (more of which later), particularly noting that the typical power increase will be double that for a normally aspirated engine. Another benefit of chipping is better throttle response (but also see carburation chapter).

So, what is an engine management chip and what sort of engine functions does it control? The chip is the brain of the engine management system and will usually control the ignition, thereby replacing a conventional distributor, and the fuelling, by controlling an electronic fuel injection system. Additional functions are controlling the ultimate rev limit of the engine and, if the engine is turbocharged, it may control absolute turbocharger boost.

An EEC IV/V Performance Power Module. (Courtesy - Superchips Ltd)

The really big power increases achieved by chipping are usually the result of the new chip allowing considerably higher turbocharger boost on a turbocharged engine, and it is this boost that produces the power increase. In other instances an improvement in engine performance is achieved by a change in engine fuelling at certain points in the rev range where the manufacturer may have set the fuelling for economy rather than performance. On the subject of fuelling and power, or turbo charging, see the relevant chapters for further details.

Fine tuning a chip performance on the rolling road using data downloaded from Superchips' main computer. (Courtesy - Superchips Ltd)

The Icon from Superchips - a re-programmable ignition computer. (Courtesy - Superchips Ltd)

Where a chip change allows more forced induction boost to be developed, you must be aware that the considerable increase in torque and power places extra stresses on both the engine and drivetrain. With most other chip changes you need to shop around for the right type of chip because some are more performance orientated than others. Additionally, if you have made significant changes to other aspects of the engine, such as to the induction or exhaust systems, the chip manufacturer needs to be made aware of them in order that the correct chip is supplied, or, as is the case with Superchips, it can be fine tuned to suit the engine modifications.

Chipping can be done by yourself, replacing the standard chip with a modified one, or it can be done by a chip dealer who may additionally run the vehicle on a chassis dyno and tailor the chip to your car. With some cars, most notably a Ford fitted with the EEC IV or V computer, the chip is not actually changed but rather a power module is plugged into the engine computer. This essentially has the same effect as chipping the computer, but works in a different way. More recently, it has become possible to have the existing chip reprogrammed with the option of switching back to the original and standard programme either permanently or temporarily.

For those cars that are impossible to chip, it is now possible to fit a secondary management computer from Superchips. The secondary management computer, in essence, allows the engine to behave as if it had been chipped, with the same benefits.

Fully programmable ECU for the MX-5/Miata. (Courtesy - Flyin' Miata)

Chapter 3
Fuel systems

INTRODUCTION

Improvements to the engine fuel system should increase engine torque and horsepower and thereby affect two aspects of performance - acceleration and straight line top speed. However, because the improvements may also include an improved throttle response and elimination of flat spots (the latter more so with engine management system changes), cornering speeds may improve also, particularly in very fast bends by virtue of having more power. The fuel delivery system has some of the greatest scope for power tuning, especially in older engines with carburettors, though fuel injected engines also have great potential. Whether the fuelling is by carburettor or injection while the modifications are 'bolt on' it will be the calibration of the fuel delivery that ensures the parts yield their full gain and this should be undertaken on the chassis dyno/rolling road.

However, before you make any decisions regarding modifying the fuel delivery to the engine you need to understand the basic principle behind carburation. Any carburettor in its rawest form can be considered as a tube that is narrower in section at one point. It is at this narrowest point that the fuel is introduced. The name for tubes with a narrower section at one point is 'venturi'. The principle of the venturi is that at the narrow section the air must increase in speed. The increase in speed causes a pressure drop, and the pressure will therefore be less than atmospheric. In a carburettor the pressure drop, which creates suction, is used to draw fuel out of a reservoir, usually via a jet, and into the venturi to mix with the air flowing through it. The mixture then travels down the venturi to the inlet tract (inlet manifold and inlet port). (Note that sometimes manufacturers and workshop manuals refer to a venturi as a choke, meaning a restriction in diameter, do not confuse this use

of the word with the carburettor cold starting device choke which is a restrictive butterfly that causes the air fuel mixture to be rich in fuel by air starvation). Fuel injection is quite different from a carburettor and does not require a venturi or suction to draw or suck fuel out of the injector because it is squirted into either a throttle body or the inlet manifold.

Fuel delivery to the combustion chamber in any engine is only ever going to be by one of two means: a carburettor or injection. In either instance, there will also be an inlet manifold, with the rare exception of some fuel injection units which fit direct to the cylinder head, and there should be an air filter. The TOP TEN options chart overleaf lists, in order of priority and, coincidentally, almost by expense, the power tuning options for the engine's fuel system. After the chart, the various options, and some 'angles', are considered in greater detail in order to educate and aid your selection.

TOP TEN OPTIONS FOR POWER TUNING THE FUEL SYSTEM

1. Fit performance air filter (with injection cold air intake system) such as K&N.
2. Have the engine/car rolling road/dynamometer tuned.
3. Fit ram pipes, if not already fitted.
4. Fit high performance inlet manifold, and have it cleaned internally.
5. Fit a high performance carburettor of equivalent size to standard item(s).
6. Fit a larger size high performance carburettor if engine power output warrants it.
7. Fit fuel injection system power boost valve.
8. Fit 5th fuel injector, secondary injectors or fit high performance fuel injection throttle bodies.
9. Check fuel line internal diameter size/bore and fuel pump are adequate.
10. Consider nitrous oxide injection and alcohol fuels.

AIR FILTERS & AIR BOXES

The air filter prevents dust, small stones and other rubbish going into the engine. The reason for filtration is that foreign bodies (e.g. rubber granules, rock salt) entering the engine will be detrimental, possibly even fatal, to engine life. Some racing cars run without air filters, but they are able to do this because they need only have a life of a couple of hours before they will have done their job and be ready for a re-build (hardly practical for a road car). In some instances, the air filter will be an integral part of a larger assembly such as an injection system, cold air intake system, or air box.

There is no reason why an air filter and associated fittings, where fitted, should be detrimental to engine performance but the reality is that they often are. Because an engine's power output is directly linked to how much air it can breathe, it follows that a less restrictive filtration system, coupled with a corresponding increase in fuel to restore the air to fuel ratio, will allow an engine to produce more power.

There are two main categories of performance air filter - foam and oil impregnated cotton gauze. There are several brands of both type of filter. My preference is for the K&N

Here is a 'Typhoon' induction kit from K&N. (Courtesy - K&N)

A high performance air filter such as the K&N item shown here fitted to a 2000cc engine and swapped into a Vauxhall Corsa will nearly always outperform the stock item.

Whether for road or motorsport always use an air filter as it will considerably prolong engine life and there will always be a filter big enough.

oil impregnated cotton filter but, whichever type and brand you decide upon, it should not preclude the use of an air box. In independent tests, high performance air filters have produced gains of 5bhp on medium size engines right up to gains of 20bhp on big V8s.

RAM PIPES (VELOCITY STACKS/TRUMPETS/AIR HORNS/BELLMOUTHS)

On some carbs or injection systems, at the entrance to the carb or throttle body is what I will call a ram pipe, though they are known by a multitude of other names. Weber and Dellorto sidedraught carbs have them as standard, whereas SUs and most downdraught or economy carbs don't. However, whatever fuel system is fitted to your car's engine, a change in ram, or the fitting of one for the first time, can yield an increase in power. In addition, the ram can improve engine response and flexibility across the rpm range, especially at the bottom end. The restriction on choice is dependent on the fuel system fitted to the engine. If you can't find what you want, it is possible to make your own or have them made for you. The best rams are the full radius (FR) type and have to be used for the results to be believed; these are widely available from manufacturers such as ITG and TWM Induction.

The next most important thing about ram selection is the length. Consider the ram length in relation to the total inlet tract length; on this point there are two very general rules to be observed - long duration cams prefer short rams at high rpm, but long rams provide the best spread of power. However, on most fast road cars it may be necessary to have to compromise on ram pipe length due to the overall space available for the installation.

TYPES OF CARBURETTOR

Before considering a carburettor swap, you need to know what type is already fitted. One way, which I regard as the best, of classifying carburettor types is whether or not the carburettor has variable venturi or fixed venturi, albeit in some cases of the latter, having the capacity for being swapped for a different fixed size. Of the two types, the variable venturi type is most likely to be an SU, or even a Stromberg. Usually, variable venturi carburettors are used in multiples in high performance applications, e.g. twin carbs, but remember that each carb only has a single venturi.

The fixed venturi type of carburettor can be divided into two sub-groups - sidedraught and downdraught. A sidedraught is a carburettor which has its venturi horizontal and the downdraught has its venturi vertical. Fixed venturi carburettors can also come with more than one venturi, e.g. two, occasionally three, and sometimes four all in a single body.

How many venturi does the engine need, & how big should they be?

Engines may have a single venturi for multiple cylinders or a venturi for

Probably the best ram pipes for the Weber DCOE are these full radius (FR) items from either ITG or TWM Induction, as shown here on a pair of 45 DCOE on a Ford Pinto manifold.

A set of triple DCOE Webers on this 6 cylinder engine actually equates to 6 venturi.

each cylinder. It's not the number of carburettors that counts but the number of venturi, so bear in mind that typically two variable venturi carburettors, say SUs, are equivalent to a single twin venturi fixed venturi carburettor, such as the Weber DCOE. The most efficient set up generally, is one venturi per cylinder if the inlet tracts are not shared by more than one cylinder. If inlet tracts are shared, then you need one venturi for each sharing set of cylinders. As far as venturi sizes are concerned, consult the experts for your car's engine type - but don't use a carburettor or carburettors with venturi any bigger than they need to be since this can lead to poor low and mid range engine performance without any gain at the uppermost engine performance range.

Carburettors are sized by the size of the throttle bore, venturi, or sometimes, by airflow in cubic feet per minute (CFM). Some carburettors have venturi of different sizes within the same body (Weber DGAV for example) so both sizes should be considered. Where the carburettor is sized by the throttle bore the measurement can be imperial inches and fractions of inches or metric in millimetres. If you are seeking to compare one carb with another by reference to size of throttle bore and the carbs are a mixture of imperial and metric then convert one set to the same measure as the other - e.g. convert the inches to millimetres.

Returning to the number of venturi, a larger number need not necessarily mean greater fuel consumption and can in fact improve matters. For instance an engine fitted with a large single venturi carb may produce better fuel consumption and lower rev range driveability when the large single venturi carb is replaced with two smaller venturi carbs (or a single twin venturi carb). Though there are always odd exceptions that may prove otherwise.

CARBURETTOR CONVERSIONS

There are two approaches to conversions: one is to fit the same type of carb but of a larger size or quantity, the other is to fit something completely different. At this point it is fair to say that although each carb type has its pros and cons, either of the two types can be made to work well on a performance engine. When you are deciding what carb to convert to, bear in mind that the final selection may be limited by available manifolds (though it is not impossible to make a manifold yourself) and engine bay space. Also consider whether it is necessary to change the carburettors at all. Will an increase in the number of venturi or an increase in venturi size, be beneficial? Is the existing carburation too small? Which type is best for the application - variable venturi or fixed venturi?

Variable venturi (SU & Stromberg)

The calibration of the fuel supply on these carburettors is controlled by a needle and a spring (SU), or needle and a diaphragm (Stromberg), and can be difficult to set up accurately across the whole rev range. That is not to say that a good dyno operator who is experienced with the SU or Stromberg, and familiar with the needle range, cannot achieve near miraculous results. The particular advantage peculiar to these carbs is that when used in very mountainous regions they remain correctly calibrated as they are self correcting in respect to air density where the air gets thinner several thousand feet above sea level. Both types are small and relatively compact, easily used in multiples and come in a variety of sizes up to 2 inch (50mm). Not least, variable venturi carbs have the edge over fixed venturi carbs at low rpm and are easier to drive on a high performance engine in slow traffic.

Fixed venturi

Of the fixed venturi carburettors, Weber and Holley are probably the

Edelbrock twin 500cfm carbs = 8 venturi for a small block Chevy. (Courtesy - Edelbrock)

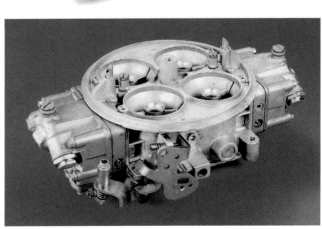

Holley 750cfm carb that can be fitted in a pair: note there's no facility for a choke on this carb. (Courtesy - Holley)

best known for high performance applications. There are, however, several makes of fixed venturi carburettor with sub classification by virtue of design. The advantage fixed venturi carbs have over SU carbs is that while the venturi size cannot be varied in operation, on some carbs it can be replaced with a variety of other sizes within certain limits (34mm to 40mm for the 45 DCOE), not least it is good for sudden full throttle openings by virtue of its acceleration jet system and thereby has the edge for high performance applications.

Progressive (differential) downdraught opening carburettors (e.g. Weber DGAV & Holley 2305)

The downdraught carburettor with progressive (differential) opening will have two or four venturi, one or one pair of which may be larger than the other or other pair (generally the primaries will be smaller). In operation what happens is that the butterfly on one or one pair of venturi opens before the other or other pair. How this works in practice is that, as the accelerator pedal is depressed, the first or primary butterfly(s) open and this opening is sufficient for the engine to run up to medium engine speeds, say 3000rpm. When the accelerator is depressed further not only is the primary butterfly(s) opened further but the second butterfly(s) on the second venturi or venturis, will be opened but at a much faster rate. Such is the speed of the opening of the second butterfly(s), both or all four reach maximum opening at the same time. The advantage of the progressive venturi downdraught carburettor is that it provides excellent economy yet has the capacity to cope with a performance engine operating at high rpm.

A pair of SU (Skinners Union) HIF model, variable venturi carbs fitted to a Rover V8.

Left, the humble Weber DGAV downdraught, on the right the performance Weber DCOE sidedraught.

Downdraught synchronised opening carb (e.g. Weber IDA & DGAS, Holley 4160)

The twin, occasionally triple or quad, venturi synchronised carburettor has 2, 3, or 4 venturi which open simultenously and is often used on vee configuration engines and in particular V6s. Although you could use a pair or 4 pair on a V8 engine you also have the alternative or using one carb with 4 venturi such a Holley or even a pair of Holleys to achieve the optimum one venturi for each inlet tract. A twin synchronised opening downdaught carb used on

V6 engines tends to be very much an economy installation and can be replaced with an installation comprising 3 similar but performance carbs. For example a single Weber DGAS might be replaced with triple Weber DCNF carbs. Something to consider when using synchronised downdraught carbs on vee configuration engines is the overall height of the installation. In extreme cases it may be necessary to have the bonnet 'bulged' in order to provide sufficient clearance for the carburettor(s).

Sidedraught synchronised opening carb(eg Weber DCOE & Dellorto DHLA)

The sidedraught Weber in the DCOE series is just about one of the best carbs you can choose to fit to any high performance engine. It is the carb seen on probably more racing engines than any other and is still eminently suited to a fast road car. One of the myths about Webers is that they are complicated and difficult to set up. In reality they have almost infinite fuel metering adjustment (calibration), albeit more expensive to do than some other carbs, and are equally at home on the shopping run as the race track. Depending on the engine installed in your car and the inlet manifold you plan to use, space may be at a premium. Because space can be so tight, particularly against an inner wing (fender), you often see sidedraught Webers used with no air filters. **Caution!** This is bad practice and almost a guarantee for short engine life - in particular, the life of the pistons and cylinder bores. It should be possible on most cars to relieve the inner wing to allow for an air filter or filter case to be fitted.

The DCOE must be mounted with rubber O ring type gaskets and flexible mountings. This is to prevent fuel

Although this is a twin venturi 500cfm Holley carb, a Weber DGAV downdraught carb with differential opening is similar in outward appearance. (Courtesy - Holley)

A Holley downdraught carb with 4 venturi (the choke only operates on two of them) but similar to the Weber DGAV in that half of the venturi (albeit twice as many) open later but are operated by vacuum. (Courtesy - Holley)

A quad Weber IDA installation, sadly lacking air filters, on this V8 engine.

foaming caused by engine vibration. Various companies market mountings that will get the job done, e.g. Fuel System Enterprises.

THROTTLE LINKAGES

If you are fitting an after market carburation or fuel injection set up you may find a throttle linkage set comes with the carb(s) or injection system

Solex carbs on a Porsche 911.

and manifold but this is not always the case, particularly with Weber and Dellorto sidedraughts carbs. If this circumstances applies, you will need to purchase a separate linkage and Weber, Janspeed, and TWM Automotive have suitable linkages.

FUEL INJECTION (FI)

Before looking at fuel injection it is worth looking at the fundamental difference between fuel injection (FI) and carburation. It's often assumed that fuel injection is a modern invention along with electronic ignition and electronic engine management systems but this is not correct. Early automotive fuel injection systems were often known as petrol injection and were mechanical systems and, of course, diesel engines had injection systems as standard fitting long before petrol engines did. The difference then between FI and carbs is nothing to do with electronics but how the fuel is introduced to the air the engine is breathing. A carburettor relies upon the venturi effect to draw fuel from a reservoir by a system of jets, into the air being drawn into the engine. An FI system does not need a venturi because the fuel is not drawn into the air flow but forced in under pressure as a fine spray. Whether the FI is electronically controlled or mechanically controlled the basic principles remain the same.

THROTTLE BODY FUEL INJECTION (FI)

Most modern cars have fuel injection systems fitted but, while offering reasonable performance, in many cases they are not designed for high performance, but rather high economy, and for a fast road or track day car they are a candidate for replacement. In other instances, it is desirable to convert from economy or even

A pair of sidedraught DLHA Dellortos (synchronised opening).

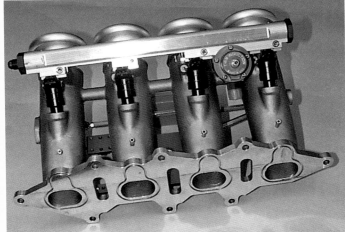

The TWM 2000 Series system injection for the Zetec. (Courtesy - TWM Induction)

Holley Pro-injection for most V8 engines. (Courtesy - Holley)

high performance carburation to performance fuel injection. The way forward is to fit what is known as throttle body fuel injection, whether the common sidedraught throttle bodies or the less common downdraught throttle bodies designed for an inlet manifold with individual runners. As with carburation, throttle body fuel injection needs a suitable inlet manifold though many sidedraught throttle body fuel injection systems have been designed to be a straight fit to inlet manifolds designed for Weber DCOE or DCNF

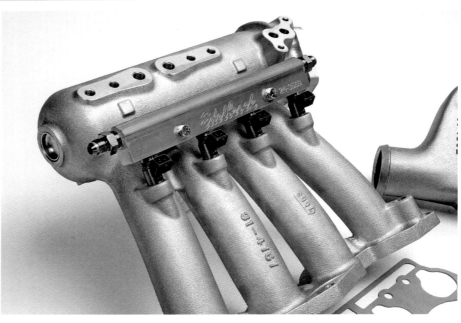

The performer inlet manifold from Edelbrock shown with secondary fuel injectors and fuel rail. (Courtesy - Edelbrock)

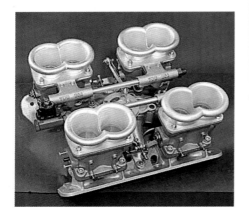

The TWM 3004 Series system injection shown here for the 308 Ferrarri but suitable to replace any Weber DCNF downdraught carburation. (Courtesy - TWM Induction)

Weber Alpha Fuel injection & ignition system shown here on a Rover V8, but could be fitted to just about anything else. (Courtesy - Weber Concessionaires UK Ltd)

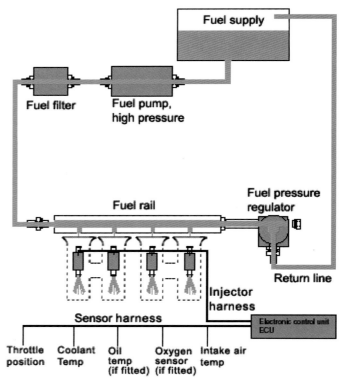

Schematic of a typical fuel injection system. (Courtesy - TWM Induction)

High performance, single throttle body for Honda from Edelbrock. (Courtesy - Edelbrock)

carbs (e.g. Ford CVH, Fiat/Lanica TC). There are also some throttle bodies designed for fitting direct to the cylinder head (e.g. Rover K-series engine).

For a typical conversion to throttle body injection the following major components will be required: manifold, throttle bodies, fuel rail, ram pipes and air filters, throttle position sensor, fuel injectors, high pressure fuel pump and fittings, and an Electronic Control Unit (ECU). Add the cost of that lot up and you come to the major disadvantage to throttle body injection over performance carbs which is the initial cost.

The advantage of throttle body FI over performance carbs such as the sidedraught Weber DCOE or downdraught Weber IDA or DCNF is that FI will be a lot more emissions friendly and can offer a lot more bottom end RPM flexibility - both

important for a fast road or track day car. As far as absolute top end horsepower goes there is no significant advantage unless the existing carburation or injection system was undersized or restrictive in some other way.

The throttle bodies themselves are available from a number of manufacturers and generally are similar though available in more than one size and, with one exception, will operate with a conventional butterfly throttle plate. An alternative to butterfly throttles will be a slide plate throttle as used on the successful Cosworth DFV Formula 1 engine; although no longer available as after market kits they can be produced as one off conversions by specialist manufacturers. The other alternative, which is readily available, is the roller body kit from Jenvey, Lumenition, or K-series engine specific bodies from Caterham. The advantage of slide or roller action throttling is the absence

of a butterfly throttle plate which is an impedance to the air flow.

ADDITIONAL FUEL INJECTORS & NON-STANDARD FUEL INJECTOR SIZES

With an existing fuel injection system it is often possible to fit an additional fuel injector into the manifold to provide a general increase in fuel supply, though this modification is not as available as it was now that better alternative solutions are available. More often, the solution is to fit larger fuel injectors and ensure that they are correctly controlled by the management chip (assuming one is used). Edelbrock's Performer X intake manifolds for Honda Civics has the facility for 4 auxiliary injectors to be fitted where pre-machined bosses exist in the design and a secondary fuel rail is also available.

INJECTION SYSTEM POWER BOOST VALVES

On an injected engine it is possible to gain mid rpm range power increases by fitting high performance fuel valves. They work by providing a higher fuel pressure than standard in the injection system fuel rail. What this does is allow a greater flow of fuel than standard when the engine in accelerated - they are the equivalent of the pump jet function of a

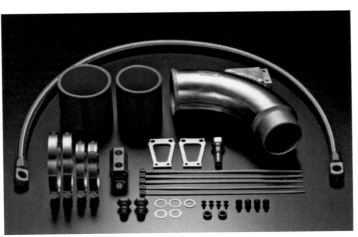

A kit to allow fitment of an additional fuel injector from HKS. (Courtesy - HKS)

typical sidedraught carb. In effect, the boost valves aid driveability and can improve acceleration.

FUEL PUMP & PLUMBING

The standard fuel pump on your car is not designed to cope with more than a moderate increase in engine power and, therefore, fuel demand, and that's assuming it is in good order. However, because a lot of cars now have a fuel pump that sits inside the fuel tank, or alternatively a cam driven pump mounted on the engine, it may not be easy to swap it for something bigger. The solution will be to fit a separate fuel pump than that can be plumbed into the fuel line, bypassing the existing pump or used in conjunction with it.

Note that some carburettors require high fuel line pressure, while others work better with high volume at a lower pressure. Be guided by the carburettor manufacturer.

To prevent fuel surges (in carburated cars), it is usually a good idea to include a pressure regulator in the fuel line. Many of these units usefully also have a built in filter.

Converting to fuel injection may require the fitment of a high pressure pump as well as a return fuel flow to the fuel tank.

INLET MANIFOLDS

Generally speaking, the manifold(s) you choose should be the least convoluted and have tracts which closely match the carburettor venturi or FI throttle bodies in their internal diameters.

You need to decide what carb(s) or throttle bodies you are going to use before you choose the manifold (in some instances you need to make the choice simultaneously). For some engines there is a wide choice of high performance inlet manifolds, and for others, virtually no choice at all.

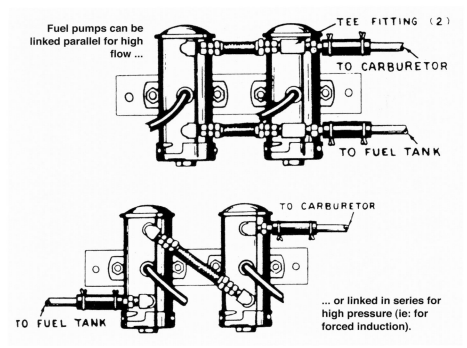

Fuel pumps can be linked parallel for high flow ...

TEE FITTING (2)
TO CARBURETOR
TO FUEL TANK

TO CARBURETOR
TO FUEL TANK

... or linked in series for high pressure (ie: for forced induction).

Fuel pressure regulator with filter.

Fuel pressure regulator without filter. (Courtesy - Rally Design)

If you are tuning a V8, you have some extra considerations to take into account because, with exceptions, V8 manifolds are divided into single plane and dual plane types. Usually, the dual plane types produce better power at low rpm than the single plane, but the reverse is the case at higher rpm. Because of this feature of V8 manifolds, you need to carefully consider the rpm potential of the engine (which means considering the cam) more so than with other engines.

Once you have your manifold, you need to consider if it needs any modification before fitting it. For instance, whatever inlet manifold you have, it is usually possible and beneficial to have an engine tuner clean the inside of the manifold, perhaps even enlarge it a bit. It is also important that the tract diameters of the manifold match those of the carburettor and the cylinder head ports so that there are no 'steps'.

If the manifold is a race bred unit, it may not have a brake servo vacuum take off. If this is the case, you will need to get it drilled and tapped, and then washed out before fitting it to the engine.

Alcohol fuels

It is not very likely that you will be using alcohol fuel in a road car on public highways. If you are, however, you'll need to seek expert advice from an appropriate carburettor manufacturer, and at least be aware that the carb will need calibrating with very large jets, must have metal (usually brass) floats and jets, and special fuel lines.

A Performer 600cfm manual choke carb from Edelbrock is similar to the 500cfm unit that will go with the Edelbrock manifold for the Rover V8. (Courtesy - Edelbrock)

Edelbrock Street Tunnel Ram performance manifold for small block Chevy. (Courtesy - Edelbrock)

Rover V8 dual plane manifold from Edelbrock will take Edelbrock or Holley performance carbs. (Courtesy - Edelbrock)

Edelbrock single plane "Torker 2" manifold for the small block Chevy. (Courtesy - Edelbrock).

Neat Performance inlet manifold for the MX-5/Miata. (Courtesy - Flyin' Miata)

Chapter 4

Nitrous oxide

INTRODUCTION

A nitrous oxide installation will increase engine power and specifically torque dramatically and thereby increases two aspects of performance: acceleration and top speed. There is a small loss in two aspects of performance: deceleration and cornering speed due to the weight of the installation, with most of the weight being in the bottle but on balance they are almost negligible.

An engine mixes air with a fuel (petrol, diesel, or alcohol) and burns it in a controlled manner to produce power. Of the air that is mixed and burnt with a fuel only approximately 20 per cent of it is oxygen and it is the oxygen that supports the combustion of the fuel. Nitrous oxide (N_2O) is a gas that has approximately half as much oxygen again (36 per cent), compared to normal air. Therefore when nitrous oxide is used to supplement the normal air used in combustion, more fuel can be burnt in direct proportion to the amount of extra oxygen that the N_2O introduces.

The use of N_2O is usually restricted to the drag strip but there is no reason why it cannot be used on a road car. However, in practice there are two reasons which make it less than suitable. Firstly, although the installation may be reasonably affordable, the running cost of having a gas bottle refilled after five minutes usage, maybe less, can make it less practical though it depends how often you want to use the extra power the N_2O provides. Secondly, the extra power being produced has to be 'handled' by the engine and that means the extra loads on pistons, rods, crank, clutch and just about everything else.

Assuming that those two negative aspects of using N_2O are not a problem, for instance you use the car to drag race at weekends, then all you need to do is buy a kit and fit it. At its most basic level, a kit will comprise a bottle and bracketing (the bottle has to be at a

Typical nitrous bottles. (Courtesy - NOS/Holley)

slight angle), an auxiliary fuel pump (not always included), piping, two solenoids and a switch/switches.

In recent years nitrous systems have developed and it is no longer the case that you have to remove the intake manifold from your car's engine to have it drilled and tapped for the N²O injector to be fitted as bespoke manifolds are available for popular engines. Also nitrous systems have developed from basic solenoid control of the N²O injection and second solenoid to control

extra fuelling to three basic types of installation which can be classified as follows.

WET NITROUS SYSTEMS

The wet nitrous system is one where both fuel and nitrous are injected together from a single nozzle, albeit still with two solenoids controlling fuel and nitrous respectively. Typically, the injector will be placed in the plenum before the intake manifold itself. Edelbrock do kits for a number of

Honda engines as well as a generic kit, that produce a typical power increase of 40-60bhp.

DRY NITROUS SYSTEMS

The dry nitrous system is one where the nitrous is injected into the plenum chamber ahead of the intake manifold. The additional fuel required to burn with the nitrous is injected through the existing engine fuel injectors with the flow rate being controlled by an interface with the nitrous system. Again, Edelbrock do a kit for a number of engines including the Ford Zetec engine as well as a generic kit.

Wet Nntrous DSstem kit. (Courtesy - NOS/Holley)

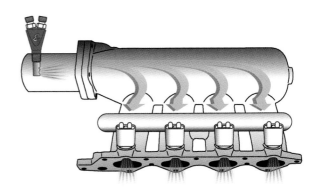

A typical wet nitrous installation. (Courtesy - Edelbrock)

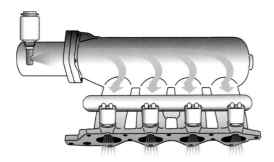

A typical dry nitrous installation. (Courtesy - Edelbrock)

Dry Nitrous System kit. (Courtesy - NOS/Holley)

DIRECT PORT NITROUS SYSTEMS

The direct port nitrous system is a system where both nitrous and fuel are delivered together, like the wet nitrous system but, rather than being delivered in the plenum, the delivery is by a nozzle into each intake port runner. Installation will require modification of the engine's intake manifold for the delivery nozzles though some performance intake manifolds from Edelbrock are available with bosses in the casting that are specifically designed for adaptation to take the nozzles. Edelbrock also do a direct port kit.

Neat direct port NOS installation by Matt Jobling on this Weber DCOE carburated engine.

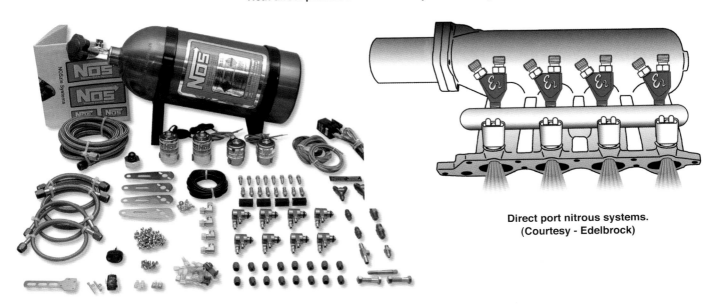

Direct Port Nitrous kit for Honda engines. (Courtesy - NOS/Holley)

Direct port nitrous systems.
(Courtesy - Edelbrock)

Chapter 5

Forced induction

INTRODUCTION

There are two types of forced induction: turbocharging and supercharging. Very occasionally, an installation will incorporate both methods. The principle of both is that the air and fuel mixture (the 'charge') is forced into the cylinders. The operating pressure is usually expressed as a barometric pressure (bar) rather than pounds per square inch (psi). Because more air and fuel is available for combustion the engine ultimately produces more power (torque and horsepower) and, generally, forced induction engines have a power curve that is strong in the low and mid rpm ranges and, unlike conventional tuning, the rpm range is not necessarily extended upwards.

Because the power is produced in those useful low to mid rpm ranges, there is no loss in flexibility until extreme power gains are sought. All of which make forced induction a good tuning option for a road car. One

particular advantage turbocharging has over many other tuning modifications, including supercharging, is that it can actually reduce the amount of noise

the vehicle produces which is very useful for a road car. Of course, if you want noise it will make it. However, I have known a turbocharged

A massive supercharger on an American V8.

46

Supercharger kit for the K-series engine Lotus Elise from Turbo Technics.

Supercharger kit complete with intercooler for the Honda Acura from Procharger. (Courtesy - Procharger)

racing engine produce slightly less noise through an exhaust system with no silencer than a similar non turbocharged engine, which was not only not using a silencer box but produced considerably less power as well!

However, every turbocharger or supercharger installation will increase the weight of the vehicle and thus reduce three aspects of performance. Clearly, the power gain should more than balance out the weight gain so that there will be improved acceleration and outright top speed, but there will be a loss of cornering speed and an increase in stopping distance.

Looking at supercharging first, a supercharger can be thought of as a pump or compressor. It is driven by the engine from the crankshaft by either a vee belt (or belts), or a toothed belt. There are a variety of different types of design, some of which are no longer in production. Of the types still readily available,

the most popular appears to be the centrifugal compressor design which looks remarkably similar to half a turbocharger. Another type is the Lysholm, or screw compressor, which tends to be a larger unit and more cuboid in shape, and on which the drive may be on an extension from the main body. The supercharger's main advantage over a turbocharger is that the extra power is available the instant the throttle is pressed without any hesitation or lag. Another advantage is that, until very high boost levels are reached, no charge cooling is generally required. The disadvantages are that engine power is required to drive the supercharger, and the unit and associated components, or a complete kit, can be expensive to purchase.

Like the supercharger, a turbocharger can also be thought of as a pump or compressor but is, in fact, two turbines. The exhaust gas from the engine spins a turbine on one end of a shaft; at the other end of the shaft is

a compressor which compresses the induction charge before it is drawn into the engine. The turbocharger's main advantage over a supercharger is that no engine power is required to drive it. Its disadvantage is that there is usually some hesitation, known as lag, before it starts to work and the unit generates a lot of under-bonnet heat.

Before considering what needs to be done to allow a forced induction unit to pass more boost to the engine, you need to decide how much more power you want. I suggest that rather than seek a power increase of a round number, such as looking for a further 25bhp, you aim for a percentage increase of, say, 10 per cent. The reason for this is that it will be easier to work within the limitations of other areas of both the engine and car. For instance, it is very easy and relatively cheap to dramatically increase the power of a forced induction engine only to find that the clutch, gearbox, and driveshafts (to mention a few

This supercharged V8 engine is fed with a single 4 venturi carburettor, the supercharger is a compressor displacement type - either a Roots or Lysholm design.

components) break with annoying regularity. This is more often the case with forced induction tuning than with other conventional tuning techniques, largely because of the increase in torque produced. This is one reason why manufacturers deliberately limit boost at certain points in the engine's rpm range.

Here is the same installation closer in so you can see the length of the supercharger driveshaft extension - different lengths of extension are available.

This supercharged V8 engine is fed with dual 4 venturi carburettors (total 8 venturi), and the supercharger unit itself is physically longer than the single 4 venturi carburettor installation.

TUNING EXISTING INSTALLATIONS

Once you've decided on how much more power you want, you can look at what is preventing the current installation from realising that amount of power and then work out a plan of action to increase power. The two options tables overleaf can be used as a guide, and the options are listed in an approximate order of power yield but it must be remembered that these

The Procharger supercharger unit looks like the compressor from a turbocharger but should not be confused with a turbocharger. (Courtesy - Procharger)

Supercharged Honda VTEC engine using the Procharger kit. (Courtesy - Procharger)

In this close-up of a turbo you can see the waste gate to the right of the turbine.

A HKS Sports Turbo kit for a Mitsubishi. (Courtesy - HKS)

This HKS GT turbocharger has been dis-assembled so that you can see, from left to right: the inlet housing, compressor wheel - centre housing - turbine, exhaust housing. (Courtesy - HKS)

are only guides. For instance, it could be that fitting a high performance dump valve may yield the desired gain in performance (not necessarily more power) without spoiling engine flexibility by introducing turbo lag, and it could be a cheap modification. Finally, with any forced induction engine, never forget that conventional tuning techniques are still generally valid. After the tables there are various sections, each of which look at forced induction high performance tuning in greater detail.

TOP THREE OPTIONS FOR TUNING SUPERCHARGED SYSTEMS

1. Increase boost pressure (by changing supercharger speed or fitting larger unit).
2. Fit a charge cooler (where possible) or a fuel cooler (where possible).
3. Improve engine breathing using conventional tuning methods.

TOP FIVE OPTIONS FOR TUNING TURBOCHARGING SYSTEMS

1. Increase boost pressure (by fitting a modified chip, modified wastegate, or both).
2. Fit a charge cooler or larger charge cooler (intercooler) either air/air or water/air.
3. Improve engine breathing using conventional tuning methods.
4. Fit a performance dump valve.
5. Fit a modified turbocharger that is optimised for the engine, e.g. not just bigger.

INCREASE IN BOOST PRESSURE

For any engine with an existing forced induction system, the easiest way to get the engine to produce more power is to increase the boost. However, this can cause problems too, for example,

by increasing the temperature of the inlet charge (more of which later). Also, with any forced induction system there are usually several factors that limit boost. Firstly, there is likely to be some kind of blow-off valve, or, more commonly with a turbocharger, a wastegate. Secondly, the size and design of the unit itself may be the limitation. Thirdly, higher charge temperatures created by increasing boost can reduce the amount of power that can be produced because the rise in pressure heats the charge. Each can be overcome as follows: the blow-off valve or wastegate can be modified or changed for a different one so that higher pressures can be attained before activation; the unit itself can be exchanged for a larger item; the charge cooling can be improved, or introduced if it did not previously exist.

CHARGE COOLING

The fuel/air mixture, or charge, can be cooled by passing it through either an air/air intercooler, a water/air charge cooler, or a larger or secondary unit if one is already fitted. Both intercooling and charge cooling do the same job, but the former uses air as the cooling medium and the latter uses water. You are more likely to find either type of charge cooling on a turbocharged application than a supercharged one. Usually the charge cooler will take the form of an air/air intercooler. An intercooler looks very similar to a radiator or oil cooler. It will nearly always be made of aluminium, and often won't be painted. If the turbocharger installation on your car's engine is not intercooled, consider fitting an intercooler as a priority. Depending on the engine and turbocharging installation in question, it may be possible to source a suitable intercooler from another model from the same manufacturer, or even from a completely different manufacturer. Lastly, it is possible to purchase a universal intercooler from a

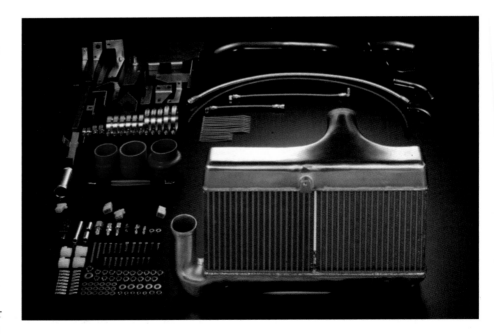

Uprated intercooler for the Mazda RX7 from HKS. (Courtesy - HKS)

HKS sequential blow-off valve. (Courtesy - HKS)

HKS sequential blow-off valve fitted. (Courtesy - HKS)

manufacturer such as Allard, Serck, or AH Fabrications, possibly even getting them to manufacture a hybrid unit for you. The same applies for installing a larger unit than standard, though you are more likely to need a unique unit specifically designed for your car's engine.

Once you have your intercooler, be it a first time fit or upgrade, it needs to be connected to the turbocharging system. Given that you are seeking to minimise the pressure drop caused by using long lengths of rubber hose (which incidentally should be silicone rubber hose), any long runs of piping should be made using large bore aluminium tubing. Samco is a good source of suitable silicone rubber hosing.

For a supercharged installation I have seen the fuel run through a small air/air oil cooler unit that reduced the fuel temperature. The theory being that if the fuel is cooler it will cool the air. The most popular way to achieve a cooler charge though, is to fit a large external (to the car body) air scoop (cold air box) to the installation to ensure the air is as cool as it can be.

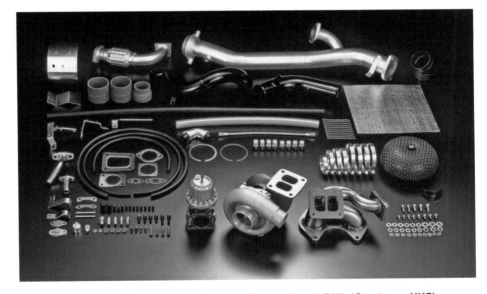

A complete HKS Turbo installation kit for the Mazda RX7. (Courtesy - HKS)

TURBOCHARGER DUMP VALVES

One well known problem with a turbocharged engine is that of turbo lag, that is, the time it takes for the turbocharger turbine to accelerate to a speed at which the compressor produces boost. Usually, this kind of lag is experienced when the vehicle is being accelerated from a low to medium engine rpm. However, it can also be experienced to a lesser extent when changing gear. The lag encountered when changing gear is caused by a build up of pressure against a closed butterfly valve in the induction system, itself created by the closure of the throttle for the gear change. This build up of pressure causes the turbocharger compressor

Turbo dump valves from Trans Auto Sport. (Courtesy - Trans Auto Sport)

Complete turbo valve fitting kit from Trans Auto Sport. (Courtesy - Trans Auto Sport)

to slow down dramatically, a condition known as stall. When the throttle is opened up again, after the gearchange has been completed, the turbo has to pick up speed once more before useful boost and, thereby, power is produced. This process takes time and is experienced as turbo lag, the turbocharger lagging behind the throttle opening. Most turbocharger installations are fitted with a dump valve that releases the excess pressure caused when the throttle butterfly is closed. If your vehicle's engine's turbocharger installation does not have a dump valve it is well worthwhile fitting one. If one is already fitted it's worth checking its functionality (leaks would lead to loss of

boost pressure) and possible upgrading to a more robust item.

FITTING ORIGINAL EQUIPMENT INSTALLATIONS TO ENGINES WITHOUT THEM & WHOLLY AFTER MARKET INSTALLATIONS

It may appear to the casual observer that the difference between a forced induction engine and its normally aspirated version is simply the turbo or supercharger unit. On that assumption it would appear that, aside from dropping the compression ratio of the engine, the forced induction parts can be bolted on to your normally aspirated derivative and the job's

done. Not so simple, the reality is that, even aside from crucial differences in the fuel delivery system, there are a lot more differences. For instance, not only may the cylinder head casting be different (as with Rover A Series) but even the block, con-rods, and a whole load of other components may be differently engineered too. Because of this complexity, it's usually easier and cheaper to do a complete engine swap - including the forced induction unit - rather than try and do a bolt on conversion using original equipment parts on the same engine. Where an engine has no forced induction derivative such as the Rover (Buick) V8, there are two approaches that can

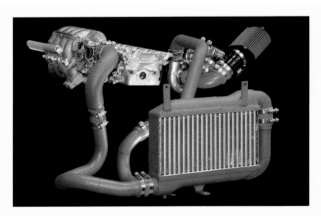

Turbocharger installation kit for the MX5/Miata. (Courtesy - Flyin' Miata)

The same turbocharger kit but now installed on the MX5/Miata. (Courtesy - Flyin' Miata)

be taken. The easiest way is to buy a kit from a reputable tuning company, possibly even having them carry out the fitting as well. The alternative is to design and build your own installation from scratch using after market components or adapted production components. In the case of the former, your contractor will do the thinking and work for you, and in the latter you'll need to seek expert advice and do your own research.

Silicone hose kit from Samco Sport on this high performance turbocharger installation.

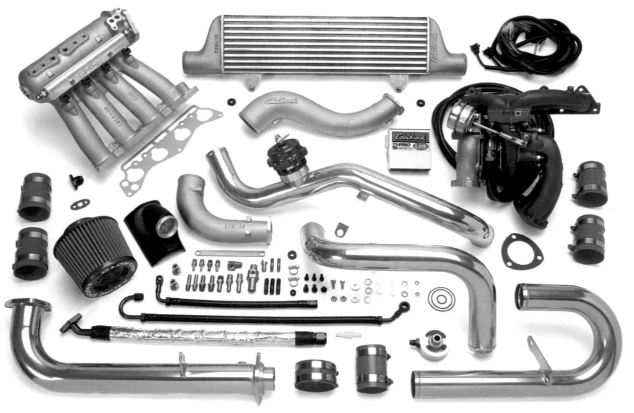

Complete turbocharger installation kit for the VTEC engined Honda Civic from Edelbrock. (Courtesy - Edelbrock)

Chapter 6

Exhaust system

The exhaust system consists of two or, more recently, three, separate components; firstly, the manifold (header) which bolts to the cylinder head(s); followed by the exhaust system which will comprise the silencer (muffler) box(es); and the more recent third component, where fitted, will be the catalytic converter which will be near the front end of the system.

The exhaust system performs two tasks. The first is removing the exhaust gases and depositing them out of the way, usually behind the car but sometimes alongside it. The second is to silence the noise made by the combustion in the engine. Modifications to the exhaust system should increase power (but can decrease it) and thereby improve two aspects of performance: straightline top speed and acceleration. However, as with all increases in power, cornering speed may also be improved upon. Less obvious are the improvements, or even detriments, to deceleration which

This Vauxhall Calibra has a Janspeed exhaust system fitted: the back box is shown separately. (Courtesy - Janspeed)

could be caused by changes in the weight of the exhaust system. Finally, because the exhaust system comprises several parts, each part is considered separately. The following table shows the top five exhaust tuning options.

TOP FIVE OPTIONS FOR EXHAUST TUNING

1. Fit freeflow exhaust system (excluding manifold/s).
2. Optimise exhaust system pipe diameters (requires expert advice).
3. Fit freeflow exhaust manifold (including CV system).
4. Consider removal of catalyst - if legal

Fiat Cinquecento Sporting fitted with Janspeed performance exhaust manifold and system. (Courtesy - Janspeed)

(for weight saving and/or improved gas flow).

5. Use exhaust manifold insulating tape (if you can afford regular manifold replacement).

EXHAUST SYSTEM

The original equipment/standard replacement exhaust system will comprise piping and silencer boxes ending with a tailpipe. It will have been designed with cost and noise reduction as high priorities and performance considerations of little or low significance (more so on family saloons than sports versions which may have a slightly better system).

The replacement of the standard exhaust system with a high performance version allows the engine to produce more power by releasing the exhaust gas to the open air more

Janspeed rear silencer box for Nissan 200SX. (Courtesy - Janspeed)

efficiently and, in so doing, reducing the pressure of the exhaust gas in the system. This is known as reducing the 'back pressure' or reducing overall engine 'pumping losses'. To understand how this works, think for a moment about where the exhaust gas is created, i.e. in the engine combustion chamber when the fuel and air mixture has ignited. Combustion produces the power stroke that forces the piston down the cylinder, it also produces exhaust gas. When the piston starts its

ascent back up the cylinder, it pushes the exhaust gases ahead of it. 'Pushes' is the key word here because the exhaust gas has to be forced up the cylinder, out of the exhaust port, and down the whole length of the exhaust system. A certain amount of energy is required to push that gas out of the system. If restrictions to the exhaust gas's passage to the atmosphere can be minimised, then less power is used to push the gas out and the power saved can be more usefully used elsewhere - like driving the wheels of the car.

One way a high performance system may achieve lower resistance is by having a larger bore (tube diameter). A bigger bore allows more gas to flow through the system. However, when a gas flows through a larger diameter pipe the speed (velocity) of the gas is slower, and too large a bore creates too slow a gas speed. A slow exhaust gas speed causes a loss of power because of the way outgoing exhaust gas in the cylinder head aids induction of the inlet charge by creating a flow of gas (it helps suck in the inlet charge). The

Jetex system for the Nova with DTM tailpipes. (Courtesy - Jetex Exhausts Ltd)

difficult part about tuning the bore size is that there are many variables to consider including the engine type, camshaft/s and rpm. All these considerations mean that though it is difficult to get a very good system optimised for your application, it's very easy to get a bad one.

How much of a gain in power a high performance system will achieve depends both on how bad, or how good, the standard system is, and on how good the high performance system is. Janspeed, for instance, usually claim a power increase of ten per cent, and often more, for their high performance systems. With that

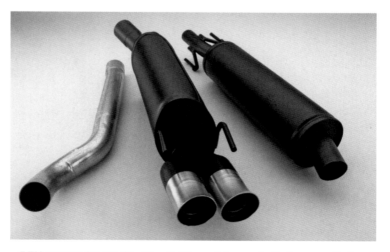

DTM system for the Cavalier Gsi from Jetex, note that, unusually for a silencer, the outlet pipes are in the opposite plane to the silencer box. (Courtesy - Jetex Exhausts Ltd)

performance gain you'll usually also get a distinctly sporty exhaust note. Bear in mind that, with some manufacturer's systems, the exhaust noise can be unpleasantly, if not illegally, loud. Something else to watch with after market high performance systems is that you only get what you pay for - a cheap performance system may be short lived.

EXHAUST MANIFOLD (HEADER)

In recent years car manufacturers have paid more attention to exhaust manifold design, and so the big power gains that you might see on changing the manifold on older cars (pre-1980, for example) are less likely to be found on more modern cars. If you find that for your particular car there appears to be no high performance manifold available, or very few, it may well be because the standard manifold is actually quite good, or perhaps because your car is unpopular for power tuning. As a guide to whether or not the manifold is any good or not, see if it is made in cast iron, as opposed to steel tubing, and how long the individual cylinder downpipes are before they join together, either in pairs or all at once. A cast iron manifold with very short cylinder runs can usually be replaced with something better. Finally, if nothing is available off-the-shelf, it is always possible to have a unique system made for any engine - at a price.

Controlled vortex (CV) exhaust manifold

A variation on the standard tubular or freeflow manifold is the Controlled Vortex (CV) tubular or freeflow manifold. The CV, or 'anti-reversion' manifold, was developed by Janspeed in conjunction with tuning guru David Vizard in 1981. At the time,

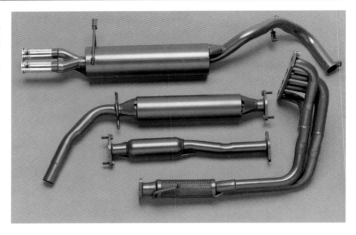

Manifold and system for the Rover Metro 16V 1400 from Janspeed. (Courtesy - Janspeed)

Janspeed seriously marketed the CV manifold and it was popular with racers. However, the high cost of the manifold made it a less popular conversion for road cars. In addition, the real benefits are not realised unless used on engines with large carburettor chokes and long period cams, these items being only found on the hottest road cars. Because of the relatively small demand, CV manifolds are made on a one-off basis and are quite expensive. Janspeed hold the British patents for the CV manifold and, because they are a volume manufacturer, they are generally not that keen to manufacture a CV manifold at all (only at times of the year when they have available production capacity).

The CV manifold is different from other manifolds in that, at its port end, it has small cones with a

Very neat 4 into 1 exhaust manifolds for a V8 engine from Edelbrock. (Courtesy - Edelbrock)

large space around them and, from the outside, this part of the manifold just looks slightly thicker. The reason for the cones is that with an engine that is running a long duration cam (the valves are held open longer than standard cam timing) there is a problem with lower exhaust gas speed and reverse flow (gas flowing back through the port and into the combustion chamber), both of which cause power loss. The long duration cam timing allows more fuel and air mixture to enter the combustion chamber, especially at high rpm, but at low rpm causes the aforementioned problems. The cones in the CV manifold hinder the backflow of exhaust gas. To quote Janspeed: "... controlled vortex manifolds are designed for competition cars running wild camshafts with high induction and exhaust gas speeds. The benefits of a controlled vortex manifold are that the engine gains torque at the bottom to mid rpm range without loss of bhp at the top end. As a byproduct of increasing torque, and hence lowering the usable rpm, you will also find that the car will become far more efficient fuelwise." In his own books David Vizard says a great deal about the CV manifold

Nicely chromed 6 into 2 manifold.

You can see the 4 into 2 joins on this manifold. (Courtesy - Edelbrock)

system but one phrase in particular speaks volumes, "the extra low end torque would be instantly noticeable on the road".

The most disappointing aspect of the CV manifold is not that it is deficient in any way, but rather that it is so underrated and so little known. A CV manifold on a road car with, for instance, a mid range performance cam and Weber/Dellorto sidedraught carburettor would yield useful driveability gains and power with it. If you consider that a road car with a performance tuned engine not only has to compromise with regard to cam selection but also carburation calibration, then the benefits of a CV system are more obvious. On a Weber/Dellorto sidedraught carburated engine the choke (main venturi) will be on the small size in order to achieve maximum flexibility required for driving in city and town traffic. The downside

to sizing for flexibility is that it limits maximum power and power at the top end of the rev range (note that peak power may occur 1000 rpm before maximum engine speed). Attempts to use the optimum choke for power may result in the car being practically undriveable because the engine delivers negligible power below 3500 rpm. The size difference between the choke for flexibility and that for power may be at least one size (more likely two). The beauty of the CV manifold is that it allows the choke to be sized for maximum power yet will still allow the engine good low rpm flexibility.

CATALYTIC CONVERTERS

Before making any decisions about the catalytic converter, where fitted, it is worth taking a closer look at its appearance and how it works. A catalytic converter looks like a small exhaust silencer (muffler). However,

inside there will be a ceramic honeycomb core or a metal foil spiral roll core which has an internal surface area equivalent to several football pitches. This core is coated with an alumina-based washcoat which provides a secure base for the catalyst coating of platinum, rhodium and palladium precious metals. The exhaust gasses pass through the core where they have a chemical reaction with this metal coating; this chemical reaction converts the gases to carbon dioxide, water, and nitrogen. The exhaust system of catalyst equipped cars will also incorporate an oxygen sensor which will be linked to the engine management system.

Very early catalytic converters (probably only seen in the USA) were of a poor design and created excessive pumping losses. More recent types have minimal or non-existent pumping losses, depending on what

You can just see the 4 into 2 exhaust downpipe joins on this Ford engine ...

... whereas on a similar engine a 4 into 1 manifold has been used.

make and model car you have. Porsche was one of the first, if not the first, to produce a solution to exhaust pumping losses through the 'cat' and came up with an alternative to the ceramic honeycomb - metal foil. The early metal foil catalyst that Porsche developed was found to have several advantages over ceramic types, including the all-important airflow capability. Porsche fitted the new style cat to the Carrera 911 model with no loss of power; it also raced cars fitted with 'cats' in the mid '80s.

After Porsche and other manufacturers had led the way, it wasn't long before after market high performance catalytic convertors were available. Of these, the Peter Maiden Sebring

cat was, perhaps, the most well known. The Sebring 'cat' had a carbon dioxide sensor connection and headshield, and was designed to fit a vast range of models. Generally, any large metal foil design of cat in a good casing will produce minimal pumping losses, and can be adapted to fit an existing exhaust system.

On certain cars there may be a benefit in fitting a performance cat. However, on cars registered before 1993, although a cat may be fitted, it can be legally removed (at least in the UK) which may achieve the same thing. A final point to consider regarding cats is that some are considerably heavier than a suitable diameter pipe of the same length, and thus its deletion (if legal) can yield a very useful weight saving.

EXHAUST MANIFOLD INSULATING WRAP

There is some debate about whether or not using manifold insulating wrap will allow the engine to produce more power (by keeping exhaust gasses as hot as possible). Some have claimed that it works, while others cite clear

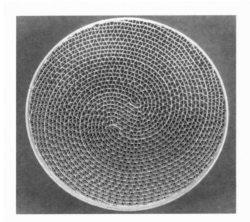

Cross section of a catalytic convertor. All of this is metal, and makes this catalytic converter a prime candidate for removal in order to save weight.

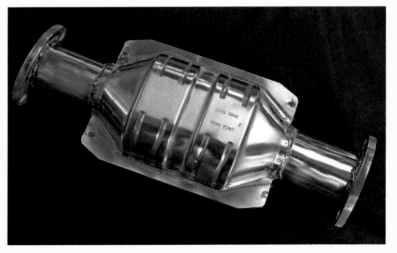

Performance catalytic converter for the MX5/Miata. (Courtesy - Flyin' Miata)

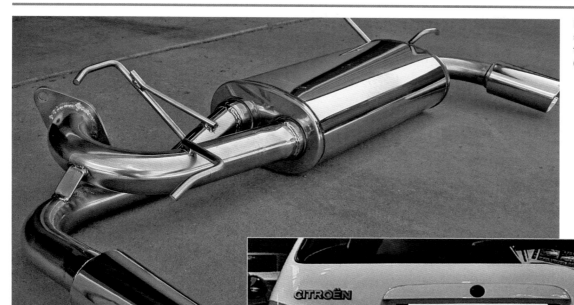

Dual tail pipes from a single line system for the Mazda MX5/Miata. (Courtesy - Flyin' Miata)

Neat side-by-side tail pipes on this Citroën - a function over fashion statement.

examples of where it hasn't. However, one area of agreement is that the use of the wrap will considerably shorten the life of the manifold by virtue of the higher manifold running temperature. For that reason alone I think that the use of the wrap is to be avoided for a high performance road car unless you have funds for regular replacement.

BRACKETING & MOUNTINGS
However you modify your car's exhaust, be sure it is all adequately mounted because, if it breaks loose and is damaged beyond repair, or just simply lost, you'll need to purchase a replacement.

Chapter 7
Cooling systems

INTRODUCTION

Performance modifications to the cooling system, as explained in depth later, may produce a small gain in engine power and thereby affect two aspects of performance: straight line top speed and acceleration. The increase in power might also affect cornering speed, and it is just possible, especially for older cars, that a change to lightweight cooling components, such as an alloy radiator replacing a copper and brass unit, would reduce vehicle weight and thereby improve braking performance as well as cornering and acceleration. However, improvements to these aspects of performance are not the main reason for modifying the cooling system, it's rather the need to have a cooling system that prevents overheating and subsequent damage to the engine.

BASIC PRINCIPLES

About a third of all the heat energy produced by an internal combustion engine has to be dissipated by the car's cooling system. Without cooling, the engine would overheat and seize. Any engine that is tuned to produce more power will also produce more heat. Note that I have used the phrase cooling rather than water cooling, as the coolant in an engine should not be plain water, for reasons I'll come onto later. The cooling properties of the oil in the engine will be dealt with in Chapter 8.

Whether you have a slightly modified saloon car, or a full engine-transplant street rod, you simply cannot afford to botch the cooling system. An automotive cooling system in its simplest form will consist of a radiator and a water pump and, more than likely, an overflow tank which can sometimes double up as a pressure tank. In other instances, the cooling system may also extend to a swirl pot. If you have an overheating problem at driving speeds of 35mph and below, look to airflow for the solution, i.e.

Complete pulley sets are available for many cars and here is a wide selection from Unorthodox Racing. (Courtesy - Unorthodox Racing)

the fan. For cooling problems above 35mph look to radiator size for a solution. The same applies if you do not have an overheating problem, but want to reduce the coolant temperature.

Having power tuned the existing engine, or transplanted another, it is now necessary to select the major water cooling components, namely, the radiator and the water pump. Dealing with the latter first, no matter what engine you are using it is extremely likely that you'll be using the standard water pump for that engine. The pump's pulley may, however, need to be altered in size.

WATER PUMP PULLEY

The water pump pulley is important because it controls the speed at which the pump will run. Changing the pump's gearing by using a smaller pulley may improve water flow at low engine speeds but can have a negative effect at high rpm by causing cavitation at the impeller - a water 'wheelspin' effect that results in no real movement of the coolant - a situation to be avoided. To reduce cavitation and improve coolant flow it may actually be necessary to fit an oversize pulley. In back-to-back tests with one particular car it was found that with a larger pulley the engine ran five degrees cooler than with the standard pulley, and that was at moderate engine speeds (because there was less cavitation and, therefore, the pump became more efficient). However, because pumps can vary so much, it's worth experimenting for yourself. Your experiences may differ.

RADIATOR

Obviously, radiator size is crucial, and not only in overall fluid capacity, but in its physical dimensions as well. In most cases, a production car has a radiator which is large enough for the worst case scenario, and still has spare capacity. On this basis, it's often possible to use the original equipment radiator for your given choice of engine and not have any cooling problems. In practice, though, three points arise: first, you may wish to run a much

Using a different pulley size can yield surprising results in cooling performance. Two sizes are shown here but there's yet a third for the same water pump fitting.

lower coolant temperature than the production model (more of this later) and, secondly, when using the donor car's original equipment radiator to go with a transplanted engine, the airflow to it may be less than the airflow it received in the original car. Finally, there may be a space constraint which prohibits the use of an original equipment radiator in the case of engine swaps.

On the face of it, assuming the original equipment radiator can cope with the additional loads placed upon it by the tuned engine, there are

no further problems. However, it's generally agreed that for optimum power and torque, an engine requires a working temperature of around 70 degrees C/158 degrees F. This is not the optimum temperature for economy (which requires a higher temperature) and the car is likely to have been designed to run at the most economical temperature. The original equipment radiator may not be capable of reducing the coolant temperature level to 70 degrees C but, assuming that it copes in every other respect (i.e. the engine will not boil the coolant), the situation can be lived with. If, however, you do want to run the engine coolant temperature at the power efficient (but uneconomical) 70 degree mark, a change in radiator, or the addition of a secondary radiator, will be required.

A look back now to the second point in our list of potential problems - that of airflow to the radiator possibly being inadequate. Quite often, the problem with airflow to a radiator is not so much getting enough air into it as getting air out. Put another way, if the air, once it has passed through the radiator, cannot leave the engine bay it cannot allow any more air to follow it. Air needs to be able to leave the engine bay easily to generate air flow through the radiator. The biggest radiator intake ducting in the world will not work if the airflow stalls once it is inside the engine bay. The simplest solution here is to cut louvres or other forms of outlet into the bonnet (hood) to release hot air from the engine bay. Another interesting solution is one passed to me by Ford Motorsport; it tells me that the air fans that provide brake cooling bolted to the front wheels of a race car also help radiator cooling by sucking air out of the engine compartment. The original Minilite wheels assist brake cooling in the same manner, though I have not heard whether they will also help remove hot air from the engine bay.

The last problem on the list was that a space constraint on the installation prohibits the use of the engine's original equipment radiator. I use the term 'space constraint' here quite loosely. It may be that the recipient car's original equipment radiator no longer fits in the engine bay because of an engine swap, or that there is simply insufficient room for the donor car's (probably bigger) radiator. The solution is to find a suitable radiator from another car, or have a radiator made from scratch.

Assuming that none of the three solutions suggested solve an overheating problem, it's necessary to engineer-in more cooling. The simplest method to achieve this is by fitting an auxiliary radiator. Of course, it's even possible to use two smaller radiators of similar size rather than a standard size radiator and an auxiliary radiator. A consideration when using an auxiliary radiator is that, like the main radiator, it must be positioned where it will receive sufficient airflow to achieve its purpose. An increase in coolant capacity on its own will simply create longer warm-up times: extra radiator area must be exposed to airflow to have any beneficial effect. Kenlowe, best known for its range of electric fans, is the only company I know that produces off-the-shelf auxiliary radiators. Naturally it also manufactures an electric fan to go with any auxiliary radiator.

A neater solution than using two radiators is to use a single, larger than standard, radiator. In this instance it

may well be possible to use a radiator from another production car that has a larger coolant capacity. If you can't get such a radiator, or prefer not to, it's possible to fit a racing radiator. A true racing radiator, manufactured in aluminium, will be much more efficient than a conventional production copper and brass (or even plastic) radiator for several reasons. The principal reason is that an aluminium radiator is likely to have a much higher ratio of water tubes per centimetre than a conventional radiator and, in itself, this dramatically improves cooling. Further, the core of an aluminium radiator is of a different internal construction, whereby it has built-in turbulators which improve efficiency, it may also have a greater core thickness. An additional bonus in using an aluminium radiator is, of course, the fact that, size for size, it is considerably lighter than many production radiators and, coupled with the customer choice of unique dimensions, it is a solution hard to fault. Specialist Serck Marston has a racing division which is a leader in the field of race car radiators, its products being found on the Jaguar XJ220 and Ford Works Escort Cosworths as well as numerous Lola race cars, to name but a few. It will also make one for your road (or race) vehicle which is dimensionally similar to, but with a thicker core than, your

vehicle's original equipment unit.

Moving on to practical things, my experience gained working with a turbocharged Clubman's race car is of interest. This car already used a larger radiator than standard, as well as an auxiliary radiator, yet still had cooling problems, largely due to the amount of horsepower that the engine was producing. The problem was such that it was not possible to use full power for prolonged periods, and certainly

For older or current models a replacement or copy high performance aluminium radiator, like the Fluidyne item shown here for a Subaru, provides additional cooling capability, and in some instances can also be lighter. (Courtesy - Fluidyne)

Fluidyne can make any radiator in any shape, size, or fitting to either your or its design - this one incorporates an oil cooler and could be on your car. (Courtesy - Fluidyne)

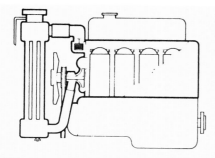

This system has no expansion tank and is filled via the radiator pressure cap. Excess coolant is vented to the atmosphere. (Drawings courtesy of BARS Products)

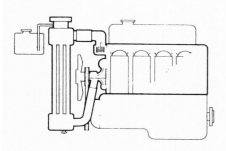

Similar to the system above except that expanded coolant passes to a non-pressurised tank. Coolant returns to the radiator on cooling.

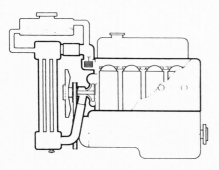

This system utilises a remote radiator header tank, identified by the connection of two or more hoses, and is filled via the header tank pressure cap.

This system uses a pressurised expansion tank with a pressure cap fitted. The tank, not in circulation, is filled via the access cap or plug, located on the highest point.

it was pointless, on that basis, to tune for more power. I approached Mel Gosney the Senior Branch Manager of Serck Marston's competition radiator division for assistance. With Mel's advice, his workshop was quickly able to fabricate an aluminium radiator which he suggested was more effective than the old copper and brass unit and auxiliary radiator put together. Not only was there a considerable weight saving, but the new unit also proved to have outstanding performance during engine testing on a chassis dyno. During this prolonged testing the water temperature never went over 90 degrees C and remained much below this most of the time. This good result was achieved while the engine was producing its best ever power figure (a substantial gain over previous dyno testing) some of the gain being directly attributable, it was thought, to the improved cooling (some changes having been made to the turbo since previous tests).

SWIRL POTS

At the start of this discussion on the components of the cooling system I mentioned swirl pots. In certain installations, steam pockets or airlocks may form in the cooling system, the latter being very much more likely when the radiator height is lower than the engine block height. In order to remove excess air from the cooling system, a swirl pot can be fitted which

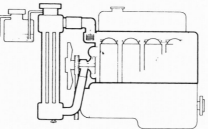

has an inlet at the top and an outlet at the bottom at right angles to the inlet. The passage of the coolant through the pot de-aerates it.

THERMOSTATS & RADIATOR (PRESSURE TANK) CAPS

Cooling systems have a thermostat in them to allow the engine to reach its operating temperature quickly by cutting-off water circulation to the radiator. Thermostats are made to open at a specific temperature which varies with the requirements of the cooling system. Although it is not possible to change the opening and closing parameters of the thermostat, it's possible to exchange it for one which opens at a lower temperature. Another option is to carefully drill holes in the body of the thermostat to increase the flow of water through it when it is open and allow some water to flow through it when it's cold. Note that the best cooling system in the world will not allow the engine to run cooler than the opening temperature of the thermostat. **Caution!** - It's possible to do away with the thermostat altogether, but this can cause the engine to run too cool as well as lengthening engine warm-up times which will increase component wear significantly. In certain instances, removal of the thermostat can be detrimental to coolant flow through the cooling system.

The liquid cooling system of the modern car engine (not air-cooled engines) is pressure controlled at the radiator or at the radiator expansion tank. The rise in temperature of the coolant itself creates the pressure, but it is the cap that controls the maximum pressure. The pressure rating of the cap is controlled by a spring. Pressurising the coolant by one pound per square inch means the boiling

These radiator (or pressure caps) look similar but have different poundage ratings - a worn spring or wrongly rated cap can cause acute embarrassment and coolant loss at traffic lights.

A thermostat (left) can sometimes be replaced with what is known as a blanking sleeve (right) but running a cooling system without either a thermostat or blanking sleeve, should be avoided since it is detrimental to coolant flow.

point is raised by 3 degrees F. Usually a system will be pressurised to 15psi and thereby raise the boiling point by 45 degrees F. Note that all this does is allow the engine running temperature to be held higher than the boiling point of water which prevents ejection of the coolant when it reaches higher than boiling temperatures. It is sometimes possible to fit a higher rated pressure cap than the standard fitting for your car if the cooling system is marginal in traffic conditions. However, this can potentially cause problems by blowing out the core (Welch) plugs in the engine block, or causing leaks at hose joints, and these are things that have to be watched closely.

Caution! - If at any time the cooling system overheats and expels coolant, never ever remove the pressure cap or depressurise the system in any way until it has cooled, as this will lead to an almost instantaneous ejection of steam and boiling liquid. The reason for this is that the depressurising drops the boiling point of the coolant, which is already at boiling point, by virtue of overriding the pressure cap and worsens the problem. All you can do is wait for the temperature to drop before any fresh coolant can be added.

COOLANTS

In most instances the engine coolant will be a mixture of water and antifreeze (usually consisting of ethylene glycol). Aside from obvious antifreezing properties and important anti-corrosion properties, ethylene glycol has a higher boiling point than pure water and typically contains anti-foaming agents, sequestering agents to prevent precipitation caused by the use of hard water, and silicate stabilisers to protect aluminium components. **Caution!** - never use water on its own as a coolant.

ELECTRIC & OTHER FANS

If you want to reduce the water temperature when driving slowly in traffic, or even when stationary in traffic, by increasing the airflow through the radiator, the best way is to fit a more effective cooling fan. In some cases more effective means larger, and in other cases, one with more blades.

Note that an engine driven fan is drawing horsepower that could be used to drive the car and thereby increase its performance. In addition, an engine fan that provides sufficient cooling in traffic is not really doing much at normal or high driving speeds because the airflow through the engine

bay is doing all the real work then. If you have a cooling problem when driving hard, it's more likely to be cured by an increase in radiator size than fan size.

All of this may make you wonder why bother changing the fan at all? The answer is to reduce the power the fan draws from the engine, and the solution is to fit an electric fan. Of course, if your car already uses an electric fan, or a fan with some type of clutch, but has a high engine temperature in traffic, then it may need a second electric fan, or perhaps a single larger fan.

You can make a trip to your local breakers yard and find an electric fan that can be pressed into service on your car. The most difficult part of such a solution will be the fabrication of brackets for it. An alternative is to purchase an off-the-shelf after market fan. There are several makes and my personal choice is the Kenlowe. The Kenlowe on my car (a second-hand purchase) must be ten years old at the time of writing and is still going strong. Kenlowe produces fans with blade diameters of ten, twelve and fourteen and a half inches, and both the smaller sizes can be used in dual applications. It usually offers a choice of fitting brackets and my experience is that the fan to body mounting, in the form of adjustable bars, is the best. This type of fitting comes with two bars and, if you need a third, Kenlowe can supply it. Once fitted, the activation of the fan can be by a thermostatic switch, direct switch, or a combination of the two.

Warning! - As many people have learned from the bitter experience of an underbonnet fire, you must always use a rubber grommet when passing a wire, or wires, through any part of the body.

The Kenlowe, and probably most electric fans, can be made to run in either direction. However, because of the pitch of the fan blades only one direction is correct. With the Kenlowe, fans are either push or suction, so decide which side of the radiator the fan will be mounted before ordering.

This illustration shows hot and cold air flows. (Courtesy - Kenlowe Ltd)

A Kenlowe 11in fan kit. (Courtesy - Kenlowe Ltd)

Another Kenlowe fan but in a larger size (13in) and showing all the components that come in a fitting kit.

Chapter 8
Engine lubrication & oil cooling

INTRODUCTION

As with the cooling system, performance modifications to the lubrication system may only produce small gains in power. However, the importance of the oil system in preventing damage to the engine cannot be overlooked.

An efficient and adequate lubrication system is an essential requirement for any fast road car. The reason oil is so important is that it is not only a lubricant but also a coolant. The more power any given engine produces the more heat it produces, which is also the case when an engine is running at a higher than standard rpm (the rpm the engine was designed to run at). Because some of that heat, such as that generated at bearing surfaces, gets absorbed by the engine oil, the oil will heat and, as it gets hotter, will gradually lose film strength. If this continues, it will no longer be able to prevent the two metal surfaces from touching, at which point seizure occurs.

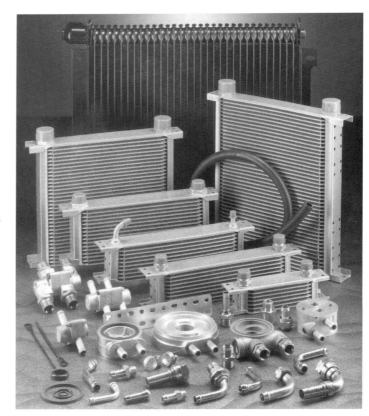

Every oil cooling component and fitting you'll ever need? (Courtesy - Serck)

OIL TEMPERATURE GAUGE

To establish whether the engine oil temperature is such that film strength is likely to be lost, it's necessary to measure it. Without an oil temperature gauge it is very difficult, but not impossible, to find out what the operating oil temperature range of the engine is. The use of a temperature indicator strip is one alternative method that can be used. However, the real and permanent solution is to fit an oil temperature gauge and further details are given in the electrics and instrumentation chapter.

OIL COOLERS

Having established the temperature range of the engine oil, if you find it is hotter than 230 degrees F (110 degrees C), the next priority is to fit an oil cooler. An oil cooler is a radiator that exchanges heat between the oil and a cooling medium; usually the cooling medium is air, but it can be the engine coolant. The flow of the cooling medium through the matrix of the cooler unit cools the oil passing through it. Fitting a cooler also increases the total oil capacity of your engine's lubrication system by the capacity of the unit you fit and its associated pipework. Before fitting a cooler the optimum size must be determined. This can be decided by reference to how great a reduction in oil temperature you are looking for.

Air-cooled units

Air-cooled oil coolers come in a variety of shapes and sizes with the most common sizes having a width of nine or thirteen inches (229 or 330mm) and a height of ten rows. All other cooler sizes will have the same width but more rows (thirteen, sixteen, nineteen, and so on). For a well tuned road car a thirteen inch by ten row cooler is adequate. For more highly tuned engines it may be necessary to use a thirteen or even a sixteen row cooler to keep the oil temperature around the 212 degrees F (100 degrees C) mark. It's worthwhile doing some research on your make and model of car to see if it is more demanding in this respect than the average. In other words, does it have a reputation for being hard on oil and/or does it tend to run hot? If either of these scenarios apply, you should consider erring on the large side for the cooler. Most, if not all turbocharged engines will have some form of oil cooler already, but if you are considerably increasing the power output of the engine you may need to fit a bigger cooler. Because an oil cooler will reduce the temperature of the oil throughout the temperature range, to prevent over-cooling of the oil in cold weather, and to assist initial engine warm up, it is very strongly recommended that an oil thermostat

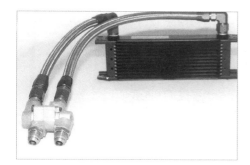

Oil cooler with Goodridge braided steel hose, fittings and a thermostat.

It's hard to be sure what caused the piston on the right hand side to suffer such damage. Later rebuilds of the engine never had the same problem but did have an oil cooling system.

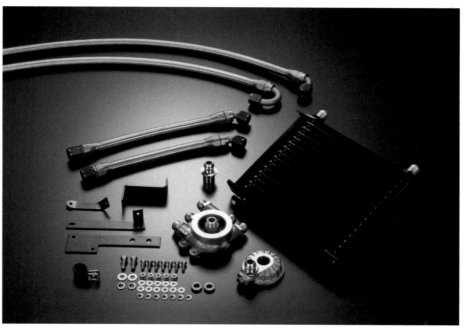

A complete oil cooler installation kit from HKS. (Courtesy - HKS)

be fitted, but more of this later.

Oil coolers are usually bought as a complete kit. Usually the kit will contain the following: cooler unit, piping, fittings and mounting brackets. A lot of these kits have universal fittings, but if a kit specific to your make and model of car is available it's preferable to a universal kit. An alternative is to buy separately all the parts you need.

Whatever cooler you have bought, assuming it is a standard air-cooled radiator type, it will need to be positioned in a good airflow. If there is space next to the radiator, that will usually be ideal.

Water-cooled units

An alternative to the more conventional air-cooled oil cooler is a water-cooled unit. The advantage with this type is mainly that it does not require siting where there is suitable airflow. The disadvantage lies mainly in the cost, which is approximately three times that of air-cooled units. If you fit this type of cooler because siting of a conventional cooler is a problem, be sure to check that your existing water radiator can cope with the extra demand placed on it. If it proves not to be coping, see the chapter on water cooling for a solution.

BRAIDED STEEL HOSE FOR OIL LINES

Generally, most off-the-shelf oil cooler kits are supplied with rubber hoses. In some instances braided stainless steel lines are offered and, if this is the case, you should opt for them. The advantage of braided hoses lies in their stronger construction and obviously higher chafe resistance. A variation on the theme is Goodridge's range of stainless steel braided hoses with coloured hose fittings, particularly if the engine will be 'on show'. If you

are using braided hoses be sure to use proper rubber-coated P-clips to secure them so that they can't move around and chafe adjacent wires/hoses.

OIL THERMOSTATS

The only drawback with an oil cooler is that, in countries with very cold winter weather, it is possible for the oil to be overcooled. To prevent this, and to reduce the length of time it takes to warm the oil, it is necessary to fit an oil thermostat. You should note that, for reasons which will become clear, you will need to decide at the planning stage whether or not you want to fit a thermostat. The first thing to consider is whether the thermostat can be incorporated into a sandwich plate (a plate with oil inlet and outlet takeoffs that fits between the oil filter and its housing). If your cooler installation does use a sandwich plate then this is the neatest solution and is recommended. If your oil cooler installation doesn't use a sandwich plate then you'll need to fit a separate thermostat unit. There is a further choice here because the unit will use either push-fit or threaded hose connectors. With threaded fittings and braided steel hose the chances of hose failure or separation from the thermostat - both with potentially expensive consequences - are considerably reduced. However, with care and regular checks, standard

Oil pressure gauge sensor, pressure gauge take off and oil union fitting.

hoses and worm-drive clip-type fastenings are acceptable.

When you come to the installation, the important thing is to find the union stub marked 'inlet' for the oil to feed into the thermostat from the engine. Likewise look for the union stub marked 'outlet' (or 'return') for the oil to return from the thermostat to the engine. **Caution!** - This may sound obvious, but if you get it wrong you could end up with a massive buildup of oil pressure and a blown cooler. The reason for failure is that when the oil is cold it will be entering the unit without being able to exit because the thermostat is in the closed position. With a sandwich plate-type thermostat you can't go wrong because the cooler will work in either direction. That said, however, a cooler may often have a preferred flow direction, so it's a point worth checking.

In-line oil thermostat fitted with Goodridge braided steel hose & fittings.

Here is a sandwich plate with an integral thermostat from Goodridge.

OIL FILTERS

There are generally two types of oil filter: the modern canister type and the older element type that fitted into a canister. The element type is always a real pain to change and invariably messy. Fortunately, for popular engines it is often possible to fit a later canister type filter in place of the original element type. Of course, there is always the alternative of fitting a remote filter too.

Remote filters

If you have done an engine swap, it might well be the case that the engine oil filter on the new engine is in just the wrong place, for instance, the space that needs to be occupied by the steering rack. The solution is to fit a remote filter in a place where there is sufficient space. However, try to keep the oil line runs as short as possible to minimise oil pressure drop, and fasten the lines in place with P-clips to alleviate any chance of chafing. With some engines, you'll need to fabricate your own blanking plate for the original filter location, for others, they are available from accessory suppliers. For those engines that are a popular choice for transplanting, such as the Rover V8, the standard pump also incorporates the filter mounting which can be swapped for a special blanking unit.

The blanking piece, which also makes it easier to plumb in an oil cooler, is available from high performance accessory and hose suppliers.

OIL SUMP
Wet type

The engine sump contains the reservoir of engine oil. The oil is sucked up from the sump by the oil pump via a pick-up pipe, passed through a filter, and delivered under pressure to all of the bearing surfaces via castings in the engine block and head (known collectively as galleries), and via drillings in the crankshaft. The oil galleries also allow the engine oil to drain back down to the sump by gravity. The sump always contains an oil reserve, even when oil is circulating to the bearing surfaces via the galleries. The reservoir has to be adequate to cope with sudden demands on its reserves, caused perhaps by a sudden increase in the oil pump's demand due to increased engine rpm. This type of system is known as a 'wet sump' system and it tends to be the norm.

Having considered the wet sump, it's helpful to think about what happens inside it when the engine is running. There is oil being sucked out, oil flowing back in, and the crankshaft is rotating at high speed flicking oil about. As a result of all these factors, the crank is running in a constant mist of oil which can actually cost a little power. Obviously the amount is small but, nonetheless, every little bit counts in the quest for power. The solution to this power loss is to dry sump the engine (more of which later), or to fit an effective windage tray. The purpose of the windage tray is to separate the reservoir of oil from the crank. There are no commercially available windage trays that I know of, so if you decide to fit one you need to make your own or approach an appropriate race engine

Remote filter with braided steel hose and fittings.

builder to have one made for you.

The sump also needs sufficient oil so that, as centrifugal forces acting on the oil, side to side (cornering) and fore and aft (acceleration/deceleration), cause the oil to accumulate in a particular point in the sump, there is still sufficient depth of oil to be picked up by the pump via the pick-up pipe. If the oil level is low, or the centrifugal forces extreme, the pump will pick up nothing but air, and oil starvation will occur with resulting damage to the bearings and, ultimately, failure of the engine (if it seizes). One way to prevent this potentially disastrous series of events is to limit the movement of the oil by baffling the sump. A baffle is a plate with some holes in it or, at its most sophisticated, one-way flap gates which prevent rapid movement of the oil without restricting the flow to the part of the sump the oil pickup pipe draws from. Flow Tech Racing Ltd produces a suitable sump baffle for the Ford X-flow engine. For other engines and sumps you may have to fabricate your own, or approach an appropriate race engine builder to have one made. Note that a windage tray can incorporate baffles, so you could solve two problems simultaneously. Finally, on certain cars such as the Mini, where the transmission gears prevent a baffle from being used, the solution is to use a special oil pick up pipe, which draws from the centre of the sump rather than from one side. For some engines, such as the Ford Pinto unit, it is possible to use an alternative and lighter sump such as the one from the RS2000.

Dry sumps

The drawbacks of a wet sump system, as explained in detail above, are numerous. A further drawback to the wet sump is that the depth of the sump adds to the overall height of the engine, with the result that the height of the engine and the bonnet line are both higher than they might otherwise be. One solution is to remove the engine oil reservoir and site it remotely from the engine - this is known as 'dry sumping'. To achieve this, a second oil pump is required, and an oil reservoir or tank must be plumbed into the system. However, the gain in power is likely to be small (single figure increases in bhp) and the cost high, though the problems of windage and oil surge will be eradicated. The system will be heavier than the wet sump arrangement without even considering any extra oil the system may require. The undeniable advantage lies in being able to site the engine lower and thus have a lower bonnet line and a lower centre of gravity. On a power tuned

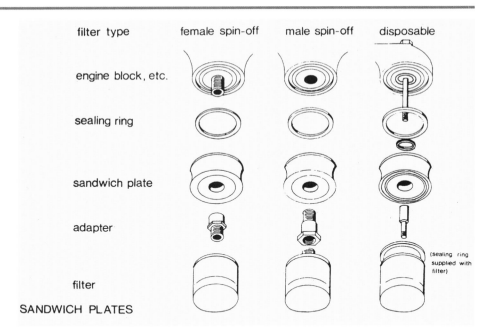

There are a multitude of available oil filter fittings and sandwich plates, as shown here. (Courtesy - Think Automotive)

road car, however, that low bonnet line may not be exploitable, unlike on a racing car where it might well be. So, on balance, this modification, although with recognised benefits, would be worth consideration only by the affluent, but even then would hardly be high on a list of priorities. Finally, many front engined, front wheel drive cars do not lend themselves to dry sumping because the transmission gears run in the sump which also acts as the gearcase.

LUBRICANTS

For high performance use, or even extending the life of the engine in normal driving, it is strongly recommended that you use a synthetic oil. You need to check, however, that it is suitable for your car.

Chapter 9
Flywheel & clutch

INTRODUCTION

High performance modifications to the flywheel and clutch centre on weight reduction and, because the parts are rotating masses, have benefits over and above any saving in mass alone. Weight savings to the flywheel and clutch improve three aspects of performance: acceleration, deceleration, and cornering (more so than you might expect in respect of acceleration).

Warning! - Performance aspects aside, there are safety considerations when modifying the flywheel.

For the clutch, modifications to increase clamping pressure improve no performance aspect, but are necessary if clutch problems and failures, due to increased engine power output, are to be avoided.

FLYWHEEL

The flywheel is fitted on the end of the crankshaft to store energy from the firing stroke of every cylinder. In addition, it carries the toothed ring gear that the starter motor pinion engages to turn the engine. Last, but not least, it provides the mating face for the clutch plate and a fastening surface for the clutch cover.

Lightening & balancing

You may have heard that lightening the flywheel will cause problems with engine tickover. There are two responses to this: (a) it probably won't, and (b) tickover is hardly important on a tuned engine anyway. The fact is that changing the cam to one with a greater overlap than standard will have a greater effect on tickover than just about anything you can do to the flywheel. In addition, if the flywheel is re-balanced, the tickover may well be smoother than with the standard flywheel.

The reason why flywheels are lightened is that not only are they a heavy mass (weight) in their own right but, as part of the reciprocating

Here is a lightenened flywheel being balanced, along with the crank, at Burton Power. (Courtesy - Burton Power)

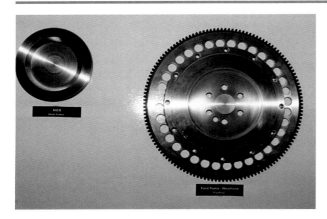

An alternative to having your car's existing - and most likely cast iron - flywheel balanced is to buy a steel item like the one shown here.

For some cars it's possible to have a flywheel made of aluminium and steel like the one for the Ford Focus shown here ... (Courtesy - Focus Sport)

... or the Audi A4 shown here. (Courtesy - Unorthodox Racing)

mass of the engine, they have to be accelerated in their own right. Less weight requires less energy to move and therein lies the improvement in performance. A weight reduction of the flywheel can be equivalent to fifteen times the weight reduction of the all up weight of the car. In practical terms, ten pounds off the flywheel can have the same effect as reducing the weight of the car by 150 pounds. But this is only the case for acceleration in first gear - pretty important for a racing start on the circuit, less so for traffic light grand prix. An approximate formula for working out the benefit of flywheel weight reduction is:

$$0.5 \times r2 \times g2 + R2 \text{ divided by } R2$$
= weight of the car lbs/1lb flywheel weight.
(r = radius of gyration. g = gearbox ratio x final drive ratio. R = radius of wheel + tyre.)

If you are lightening the flywheel yourself note that the most important place for the weight to come off is at the outer radius rather than the centre. **Caution!** - Also, note that although you may wish to lightly reface the clutch mating face of the flywheel, a serious removal of metal here will cause problems with clutch

set up heights and is, therefore, to be avoided.

Balancing is beneficial because it reduces vibration and stresses on the engine. **Warning!** - It is not unknown for unbalanced flywheels to disintegrate; this can also happen with poorly or excessively lightened flywheels. Parts of a disintegrating flywheel can tear through the bellhousing and bodywork like shards from a grenade.

Steel flywheels

Most flywheels are made of cast iron, the drawback to this material is that it places a limitation on how much the flywheel can be lightened before it is liable to disintegrate in use. Also, a cast iron flywheel can disintegrate, even when balanced, if very high rpm is used. On this basis it is a good idea to switch to a steel flywheel that has a greatly reduced risk of disintegration (almost nonexistent) and has greater potential for lightening. The only negative aspect to using a steel flywheel is that it is more expensive than a cast iron one. There are a variety of tuning companies that can supply you with a steel flywheel, but if you are tuning an unusual engine and are having trouble locating one then Farndon Engineering can make you one.

Aluminium flywheels
Although a steel flywheel can be made lighter than a cast iron one, a lighter option again, however, would be an aluminium one. However, the term is slightly deceptive because, in reality, an aluminium flywheel will have a steel centre as the clutch friction face. Alloy units are not as widely available as steel flywheels.

CLUTCH
If your car's engine is modified and producing more power, especially more torque, than the standard

engine, you will almost certainly need to change the clutch to an uprated item, assuming one is available. If your car's engine power output exceeds the design parameter of the clutch, failure can be in any one of a number of ways. Clutch slip is likely to be the most common failure and may well be accompanied by a strong smell of burning (the slip causes the clutch plate friction material to overheat). Total failure of the plate may also occur, even to the extent of complete disintegration which, in some instances, can also damage the flywheel.

Uprated clutches in organic material

AP Racing has an excellent range of uprated organic material clutches for road and race use. It can also advise you if any modifications are required, such as machining of the flywheel, before you try fitting the uprated clutch. Note that a racing clutch can be used in a road car but it will be very 'positive', and unsuitable for driving in traffic, let alone a stop-start traffic jam.

The AP uprated units are based on the standard original equipment Borg and Beck item. AP Racing produces a handy booklet which details uprated options to replace standard components. When you are considering an uprated clutch, it's important to consider the use the clutch is going to be put to, as well as the power it is expected to handle. As far as the actual power output is concerned, it's the torque rather than horsepower of the engine that must be considered. For some engines only an uprated plate is available, for others an uprated cover is available too.

A cutaway view of the same AP Racing DS series clutch, also showing engaged and released positions. (Courtesy - AP Racing))

'DS' TYPE COVER ASSEMBLY

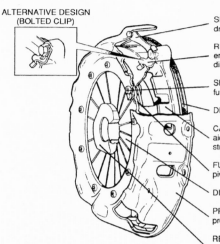

ALTERNATIVE DESIGN (BOLTED CLIP)

SPRING STEEL STRAPS- Of tempered steel to transmit the drive from the cover to the pressure plate.

RETRACTOR CLIPS- Secured by rivets, or alternatively bolts ensure that the pressure plate remains in contact with the diaphragm spring during actuation.

SHOULDERED RIVETS- Secure the diaphragm spring and fulcrum rings inside the cover pressing.

DRIVEN PLATE.

CAST IRON PRESSURE PLATE- Of ample proportions to aid heat dissipation, it is driven and located by the steel drive straps.

FULCRUM RINGS- Support the diaphragm spring and act as pivot points when the clutch is actuated.

DIAPHRAGM SPRING- Located by shouldered rivets.

PRESSED STEEL COVER- The bolting lands and holes provide ample ventilation.

RELEASE PLATE- Provides a surface for the release bearing or may be supplied without this item and used with ball release bearings.

Components of an AP Racing DS Clutch which is a suitable performance clutch for a road car. (Courtesy - AP Racing)

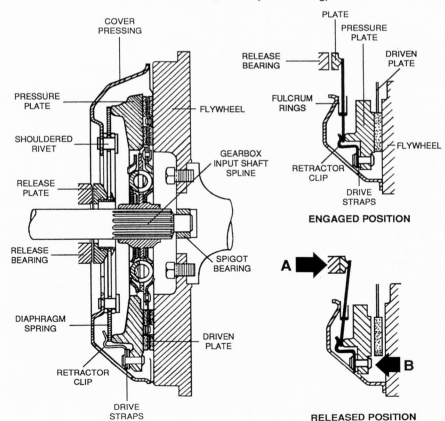

ENGAGED POSITION

RELEASED POSITION

Organic clutch plate, release bearing and clutch cover. (Courtesy - Rally Design)

A closer look at the organic clutch plate which is generally has a sprung centre as shown here. For some rare applications it can have a rigid centre. (Courtesy - AP Racing)

This paddle clutch plate has a rigid centre and should not be used unless a sprung centre paddle plate is not available. (Courtesy - AP Racing)

Paddle clutch plate can be either sprung centre or rigid centre, this one is the sprung centre and suitable for handling large amounts of power, but is not a suitable road clutch other than as a last resort. (Courtesy - AP Racing)

Paddle clutch plate

If an engine is highly tuned and burning out clutches, and it's not possible to modify the flywheel to take a larger diameter organic plate the next step - an extreme one for a road car - is to fit a paddle clutch, or more precisely, a paddle clutch plate. It is a plate that is fully circular but with contact patch areas of friction material each approximately the size of a brake pad. There will usually be four contact areas or 'paddles', but sometimes as few as three. The friction material is metal-based as opposed to conventional organic friction material. The rest of the plate is sometimes solid and undamped, or sometimes fully damped, as is the case with most organic material plates. The paddle plate is not as smooth as a conventional clutch, being very much in or out, and therefore needing a lot of slipping when driven in stop start conditions (heavy traffic). The action can be less fierce if a conversion is used that uses twin plates, but this will require a completely different clutch cover.

Metal (cerametallic) clutch plate

The metal clutch plate is a single disc of cerametallic material, and is really only suitable for racing cars. The action is very much in or out with nothing in between. It is also undamped, but does have the virtues of being extremely

This sintered metal rigid clutch plate is even less suitable than a paddle plate for a road car unless you never, ever, have to drive in traffic. (Courtesy - AP Racing)

lightweight and almost indestructible. If you have gone so far with a road engine as to need this type of clutch plate, you've gone too far with your high performance tuning.

CLUTCH ACTUATION MECHANISM

You are unlikely to come across much in the way of clutch operation problems. However, once you start to use modified flywheels and clutches, you can come across problems with

travel. The answer is to consider the method of actuation and adjust it accordingly. This is straightforward for an adjustable cable operated clutch but is more difficult for an hydraulic one.

If you have problems, it is possible with an hydraulic clutch to modify the length of the operating rod to get the travel right. The alternative is to vary the size of the clutch master cylinder, which will not only alter the length of travel at the pedal end, but also pedal pressure.

Chapter 10

Gearbox

INTRODUCTION

Because the gearbox is essentially a torque multiplier, and because torque makes acceleration, acceleration is the aspect of performance most affected by gearbox tuning. That aside, an engine swap may open up a choice of gearbox, as is the case when fitting the Rover V8 engine. On the other hand, there may be a lighter or more performance orientated gearbox available that would be worth fitting in place of the standard item. On that basis it is possible to improve one, two, or even three aspects of performance.

Gearboxes fall into two clear groups for the purposes of this chapter: manual and automatic. Of course, there are such things as continuously variable transmission (CVT) boxes, but there is not much you can do with them by way of modification, and they

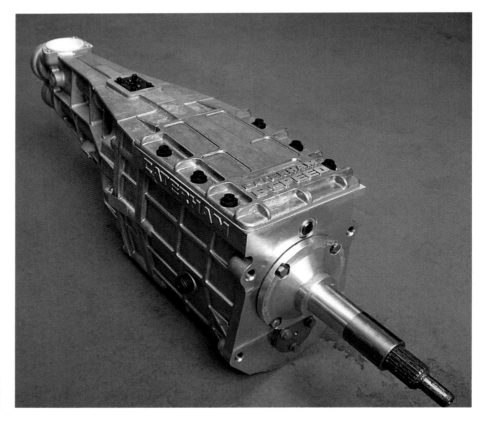

The more ratios the better; 6 from Caterham and in most Fords if your wallet can take the strain. (Courtesy - Caterham)

are not performance orientated at the present time.

CLOSE RATIOS - WHO NEEDS THEM?

A gearbox exists to multiply the torque (turning force) of the engine, and it is the ratio size and overall number of ratios that are the key to unlocking the power of the engine. In case you are sceptical about the importance of gears, when next out for a drive just try accelerating in too high a gear or using every other gear on the way up through the gear ratios. Which is quicker?

Having established how important the gears are, it's equally important to consider the ratios in conjunction with the overall gearing of the car, which means including the final drive or differential (diff) ratio in the calculations. Most gearboxes will have four or five ratios, plus reverse, and the occasional box will be equipped with six forward ratios. However, it is not necessarily the case that you need more gears to go faster. Rather you need closer ratios in order to accelerate faster. To find out why this is the case you need to consider the engine. Every engine produces power and, more especially, torque in relation to the speed it is running at. This power output can be plotted on a graph as power output against engine

Excellent for the race track, but straight cut gears - shown here in a Tran-X Ford box - are noisy and expensive for road use.

speed (rpm). The plot will look like a mountain in that it starts at nothing, climbs up to a peak or even a plateau and then drops again. Depending on the engine and how it is tuned, this 'mountain' may be steeper, narrower, or whatever, and the same can be said to apply to the power band of the engine. For instance, a highly tuned racing engine may be said to have a narrow power band, and this is where the gearbox comes in. In order to keep the engine operating within its optimum and narrow power band, it needs different gears. As the car accelerates, and engine speed rises, another gear is selected that will ideally drop the engine speed such that it is now once more below the maximum speed

(rpm) of the engine, but still at a point in the power band where useful power is produced.

If you have followed that explanation you will have realised that the narrower the power band of the engine the greater the requirement for closer gears will be if the engine is to be kept working within its power band. Likewise, the broader spread the power of the engine is, the less important close gear ratios are. Unfortunately, conventional power tuning usually reduces the power band of the engine. I say conventional because the exceptions are forced induction (turbo and supercharging) and use of nitrous oxide injection.

Looking at the ratios your car's gearbox has, there is one ratio which nearly always remains the same (usually fourth gear) with a ratio of one-to-one, even on five or six speed gearboxes. The exceptions are usually to be found on racing gearboxes and other special boxes. The one-to-one

An extra special Ford box courtesy of Flow-Tech Racing.

gear is the one gear that generally remains the same when the gearbox ratios are changed and, given that to be the case, it is apparent that for the ratios to be closer, the bottom three gears, and fifth gear if you have one, need to change in size to get closer to the one-to-one ratio. What this means in practice is that each gear below the one-to-one gear gets larger, and fifth may get smaller, but frequently stays the same. This has a drawback in that first gear ends up being quite a bit higher than standard on a close ratio box. This is no problem on a racing car where first is often only used for starting, and then with a low overall gear ratio by virtue of the associated diff ratio. An overly high first gear does, however, become a problem for a road car, and more so if you have to do any amount of city driving because you can end-up having to use excessive clutch slip whenever starting from stationary, resulting in short clutch life. The problem is, of course, exacerbated by a highly tuned engine with that little bit less power at the bottom end of the rev range.

You will realise that the more highly tuned the engine is, the narrower the power band and the greater the need for close gear ratios, but with the associated problem that it will be more difficult to set off from stationary. The reality is a bit less grim, and even moderately closer gear ratios than standard bring improvements in acceleration and driveability.

CLOSE RATIO & OTHER RATIO CONVERSIONS

For some popular gearboxes there are a wide range of alternative ratios available, for others nothing may be available at all. Some of the Ford four and five speed gearboxes (e.g. especially the Type N or 9) are very well catered for by BGH GearTech,

A look at the inside of this HKS modified box. (Courtesy - HKS)

A closer look at a 6 speed gearset from HKS; note the gears are helical cut. (Courtesy - HKS)

Quaife, TranX and other companies. You'll need to consult marque specialists to find out what is available for your particular application.

CALCULATING RPM DROP FOR ANY GIVEN GEAR RATIO

You will find details of how to calculate vehicle speed for any given tyre/rear axle combination in the Chapter 11. However, if you want to work out the rpm drop for any given gearchange there is an easy way.

To calculate the rpm drop from first to second gear divide the first gear ratio by the second gear ratio. Next, use that figure to divide the changepoint rpm figure, this gives you the rpm drop. For example,

on a standard Ford Sierra gearbox changing from first to second gear at 6000rpm we can calculate 3.65 (1st gear) divided by 1.97 (2nd gear) = 1.852 and dividing this figure into our chosen rpm produces 3239rpm. This is a useful formula when you are choosing the camshaft for your engine because you know that with the standard gearbox you need a cam that has a powerband that is broad enough to cover at least 3239rpm and preferably with some margin. However, if you have a close ratio gearbox, you can probably afford to compromise less on the camshaft. For example, staying with our Sierra, but with a BGH Gear Tech gearbox sporting close ratios of first 2.92 and second 1.865, we have a rev drop at 6000rpm of 3833rpm - a reduction of about 600rpm over the standard ratios. Although 600rpm doesn't sound much in the great scheme of things, it can be the difference between the engine staying 'on the cam' and pulling, or chugging up the revs until it is back in the powerband. The difference in day-to-day driving is significant, especially with a 'cammy' engine. Engine camminess aside, the closer ratios will keep the engine performing in its strongest range, which considerably improves acceleration.

GEAR TYPES

In gearboxes there are two types of gear in use: straight cut and helical cut. Straight cut gears absorb less power than helical gears, but are much noisier. Helical cut gears absorb more power than straight cut gears but are much quieter. From these simple facts you can see why straight cut gears are used in racing cars, where power counts for everything, and no one minds about the noise. On a fast road car, noise does matter and, even with all the sound deadening material in the world, you wouldn't want to drive far in a car equipped with straight cut gears. On that basis, straight cut gears are an example of what is good for the race track but bad for the road.

DOG BOXES

Dog boxes are for racing cars and use a form of gear engagement synchronisation known as 'dogs'. The dogs replace the conventional synchromesh mechanism.

CONVERSIONS & CASING SWAPS

You may be looking to use a nonstandard gearbox in your car for a variety of reasons, such as: the standard gearbox is too weak for projected power output, or is only a four speed and you want a five speed, or the engine you are planning to use can be fitted with a better gearbox. For instance, if you have a Ford Escort with a Pinto engine you might want to use a Sierra five speed 'box, or a derivative. An alternative would be to use the Cosworth T-5 Borg Warner 'box. Some standard boxes can be improved upon by re-casing the 'box in a lightweight alloy case that is not only lighter but stronger than the standard cast iron unit: the prime example is the Ford type nine 'box (as fitted to the Sierra). In this case, and for most Ford based conversions, the company to look to is Quaife. There is also a conversion from Dellow Automotive which will allow the T-5 box to be used with the Chevy V8.

Guy Croft Tuning Ltd does an adapter plate that enables the Ford Type 9 or T-5 Borg Warner box to be used with the Fiat/Lancia twin cam engine.

FOUR WHEEL DRIVE CONVERSIONS

Any four wheel drive conversion is going to be difficult, and it is usually less complicated to use the whole engine and four wheel drive assembly in one go, whatever it has come out of. An exception, if you are using a Range Rover four wheel drive, is that you can hang a Chevy V8 on the front of it with a special Dellow conversion.

QUICK SHIFT LEVERS & SHORTER GEARSHIFT LEVERS

For a variety of popular makes and models, including Fords, BMWs and the classic Mini, it's possible to replace the standard gearlever (and linkage where applicable) with parts that produce a much faster gearchange. The quicker gearchange can significantly improve the car's overall acceleration. The parts are usually a direct swap for the standard parts and, once fitted, are an absolute delight to use.

If you have limited funds that don't stretch to a quick shift, a simple and cheap, but second best, alternative is to shorten the existing gearshift lever so that it readily falls to hand. How much you will need to shorten the lever will depend on your seat, seat position, and arm reach. You should be aware, however, that shortening the lever reduces the leverage it provides and, in some cases, this can make the change heavier, though not necessarily slower.

You can approach the job in one of two ways. Either cut the lever in two, remove the amount you want the lever shortened by, and then weld the two halves back together. Alternatively, cut the amount you want the lever shortened by off the top of the lever and then re-thread the 'new' top. The selection of method is dictated only by the tools and equipment at your disposal.

AUTOMATICS

An automatic gearbox is one which,

Quick shift for the Ford Focus from B&M. (Courtesy - B&M)

Also a quick shift, but completely different in appearance, is this B&M shift for a BMW. (Courtesy - B&M)

instead of having a clutch and flywheel with a conventional gearbox, has a drive plate (flex plate) which also carries the ring for the starter motor to engage for starting, and a torque converter with a special design of gearbox where gear ratios can either be manually selected or are automatically selected according to preset variables the automatic box recognises, e.g. engine rpm, road speed, throttle position.

Generally, an automatic gearbox is not a performance option other than for very large engines, for instance an American V8. There are, however, a couple of things that can be done to improve performance of an automatic gearbox.

Firstly, for a wide range of automatic gearboxes there is a range of performance quick shift gear selecter mechanisms available.

Next, consider the torque converter stall speed, which is neither designed for a fast road car or engine modifications. A modified torque convertor will ensure that higher rpm can be used when the engine is in gear and held on the footbrake (known as

the stall speed) and this will enable a more rapid start when the brake is released. In fact, with a modified engine a higher stall may be necessary if power tuning has reduced the engine torque at low rpm, even though it is ultimately much greater at high rpm. Not least, it is possible to get an uprated drive plate that is stronger and more rigid than a standard item.

Automatics often have what can be termed a 'lazy' gear change which ultimately results in slower acceleration compared to an equivalent manual gearbox car. It's possible to eliminate that lazy gearchange for a sharper shift by fitting what is described by B&M as an improver or tranpack kit, or even modify fundamental characteristics of the box, such as the road speed at which 1st gear can either be re-engaged or the rpm any gear can be held to.

Final modifications for automatic gearboxes are to prevent premature failure of the unit or its components by ensuring the operating transmission fluid is kept cool and there are both cooler kits and larger capacity oil sump units available.

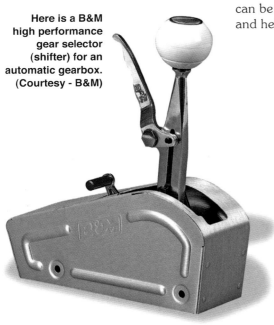

Here is a B&M high performance gear selector (shifter) for an automatic gearbox. (Courtesy - B&M)

This B&M automatic gearbox sump (pan) provides additional oil capacity and therefore more cooling. (Courtesy - B&M)

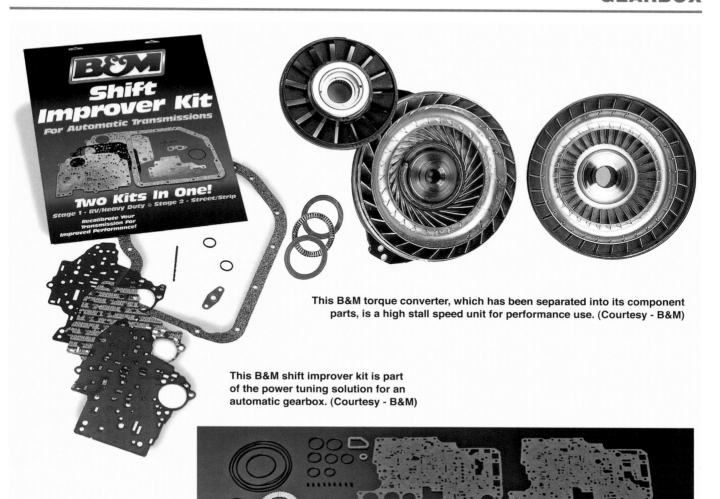

This B&M torque converter, which has been separated into its component parts, is a high stall speed unit for performance use. (Courtesy - B&M)

This B&M shift improver kit is part of the power tuning solution for an automatic gearbox. (Courtesy - B&M)

Performance auto box parts from HKS. (Courtesy - HKS)

Chapter 11
Drivetrain

INTRODUCTION

Performance modifications to the drivetrain will change two, or perhaps three, aspects of performance, depending on the modification(s) and the effectiveness of the existing drivetrain parts. Changes to the overall gearing can increase, or even decrease, the straight line top speed. A change from an open type of differential (which is the conventional fitting) to a load/speed limited slip differential (LSD) or fitting a viscous coupling (where this is possible) may improve acceleration and perhaps improve cornering speeds as well - it depends if traction is a problem. Aside from the aspects of performance, it's important to ensure that the vehicle's drivetrain doesn't break, and has the right final drive ratio for the use the car is being put to, taking into consideration anticipated changes to the overall wheel and tyre diameter.

Before considering any drivetrain modifications, you need to find out what the existing drivetrain configuration is on your car. It will be one of the following: front wheel drive (FWD) with the engine at the front, rear wheel drive (RWD) with engine at the front, middle or back, or four

wheel/all wheel drive (4WD/AWD) with the engine at the front or the back. All of these types of drive configuration will use driveshafts (axleshafts) to transmit the power to the wheels. However, if the car is RWD with the

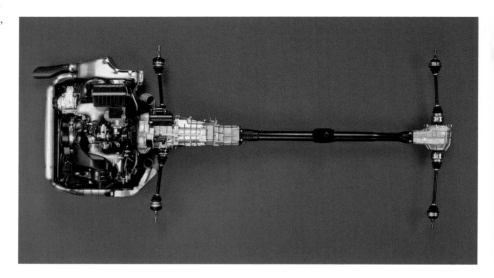

An unusual drivetrain configuration - 4WD with the engine at the back on this Porsche 911 Carrera 4. (Courtesy - Porsche)

engine at the front and has a live axle, which is a rigid axle case with the driveshafts contained within it, the driveshafts are usually known as 'halfshafts'. On a 4WD/AWD vehicle, driveshafts are usually much the same as other configurations, the main difference being that some 4WD/AWD configurations will have as many as two or even three differentials, more of which later. Once you have established what the drivetrain configuration is on your car you can begin to consider the modification options.

PROPSHAFT

Only front engine RWD or 4WD/AWD cars will have a propshaft in the drivetrain configuration, and its purpose is to transmit power from the engine to a final drive unit (RWD) or centre diff (4WD/AWD). A final drive unit includes a differential and, in most cases, a final drive ratio as well. The propshaft may be in one piece with a universal joint at each end, or it may be in two sections with a central bearing. Whatever form it takes, the most important thing is to ensure that it is in good order and have it overhauled if it isn't. Once you have a propshaft in good order, and assuming it is lubricated as necessary, it will be unlikely to break or give any kind of

problem. The only thing you can do to it from a high performance point of view, is to have it balanced by an expert company such as Reco Prop.

HALFSHAFTS

As mentioned earlier, halfshafts are the driveshafts used in live axle cars. If you have a car that has been power tuned to any extent, it is likely that the increased torque will damage the standard halfshafts. What usually happens is the shaft breaks, though it may twist first. If the shaft breaks there is generally significant damage to the differential, and extraction of the broken portion of the shaft can require complete disassembly of the unit. There are two ways to avoid this scenario: the first is to first have the shafts crack tested and, assuming they are OK, then have them heat treated to make them stronger; the second is to purchase stronger halfshafts from a company such as Quaife. If no uprated shafts are available for your car, then Quaife can manufacture a pair for you in a suitable steel, by using one of your car's old shafts as a pattern. A point to note is that if you are upgrading your car from an open differential to a limited or torque sensing type, the halfshaft will be under greater stress by virtue of the loaded wheel being

under greater load, so the strength of the halfshaft needs to be considered - more on diff action later.

DRIVESHAFTS

Just like halfshafts, driveshafts can break or twist when subjected to torque that is beyond their design limit and everything that applies to halfshaft can apply to driveshafts. They can also bend under load or mistreatment. The solution, again, is to buy uprated units from Reco Prop or a similar manufacturer.

FINAL DRIVE RATIO

Perhaps the most important decision to make when modifying the drivetrain, is what final drive ratio to use. The final drive ratio is governed by the ratio of teeth on the differential crownwheel to those of the differential pinion. The limitation here is likely to be what is available for the final drive unit you are using, or perhaps any final drive assembly that can be swapped from another model from the same

It's time for competition quality halfshafts when the spline on the standard one twists like this (middle) before failing completely (left).

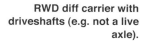

RWD diff carrier with driveshafts (e.g. not a live axle).

manufacturer. In certain instances it is also possible, within certain limits, to have a specialist gearcutter make up a crownwheel and pinion in the ratio you desire. Before you make this choice, or perhaps in conjunction with it, you need to have decided upon the gear ratios for the car and have an idea of what top speed you are aiming for (be realistic), and what engine rpm is required to achieve the desired speed. Note that modern production saloons tend to have very high final gearing in order to be economical at motorway cruising speeds at the expense of acceleration. If your car has a 5 speed gearbox or plan to upgrade from a 4 speed to 5 speed, life is a bit easier. The reason is that most fifth gears are designed for high mph - low rpm cruising. If you are prepared to sacrifice that economical cruising you can end up with a much quicker accelerating car. First, you will need to be able to work out the effect of ratio changes using the following formula:

60,000 divided by final drive ratio x wheel revs per mile = mph per 1000rpm in top gear (assuming top is 1 to 1)

To calculate miles per hour in gears other than 1 to 1 you multiply the top gear mph by 1000rpm and divide by the relevant gear ratio.

Note that you will need to contact your tyre dealer to obtain the wheel revs per mile (wrpm) figure for your chosen tyres.

Assuming wrpm of 820 (195/60 VR14 tyre) on, say, a Lancia Thema Turbo we get:

60,000 divided by 820 x 2.95 = 24.804

Dividing by 3.75 for 1st gear =

6.614mph per 1000rpm

2.235 for 2nd gear = 11.098mph per 1000rpm

1.518 for 3rd gear = 16.339mph per 1000rpm

1.132 for 4th gear = 21.911mph per 1000rpm

0.928 for 5th gear = 26.728mph per 1000rpm

A point to remember when choosing a final drive ratio is that a numerically high number is actually a lower final drive ratio. If you don't know exactly what any final drive ratio is, it can be calculated by counting the number of teeth on the crownwheel and dividing that number by the number of teeth on the pinion. For example: 41 teeth on the crownwheel divided by 11 teeth on the pinion produces 3.727. What the ratio actually means is that the gearbox output shaft turns 3.727 turns for each revolution of the wheels.

DIFFERENTIALS

With the best will in the world, not to mention tyres, your average car is always going to struggle to put down all its available power through 2 or even 4 wheels, at the same time, and especially mid-corner. The simple reason for this is that the differential doesn't allow it, and that goes for four wheel drive cars (4WD) that can have 3 diffs - one for each pair of driven wheels and one for the split, front to rear.

When a car is turning a corner, the outside wheel has to travel further than the inside wheel and, in practice, it achieves this by turning faster. The drive from the engine to the wheels in modern cars is always to both driven wheels, whether the car is FWD or

A typical crownwheel and pinion - this one is for a Ford English axle and is in steel. (Courtesy - Rally Design)

An open (standard) diff assembled with the CWP in a diff carrier.

The same CWP and diff carrier but with a Quaife Torsen diff.

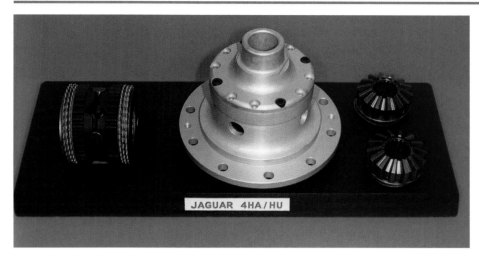

Anatomy of a clutch plate limited slip diff - this is the Gripper for older Jaguar cars and shows from the left - the clutch pack assembly, the diff carrier, and the bevel or side gears.

RWD, and to all 4 wheels in a 4WD/AWD drive car. However, the driven wheels need to turn at different rates when the car is turning a corner, otherwise the outer wheel (which is travelling further than the inner wheel) would tyre scrub and single wheel wheel-spin.

The solution is a mechanical system of sun and planet gears which can allow one wheel (or in a 4WD/AWD a pair of wheels) to turn faster than the other when it needs to, but also allows both wheels to turn together the rest of the time, all things being equal. Of course, all things are not always equal, especially when one wheel is more lightly loaded than another due to cornering forces and body roll. The differential is 'dumb' and allows the power passing through it to always take the course of least resistance and that means the wheel with least grip. Ultimately, the wheel with least grip spins progressively faster, since once it is spinning it has no grip and the diff is happy to feed all the power to it, taking the course of least resistance. That spinning wheel, which

isn't gripping, causes a general loss of momentum until grip is regained and momentum is reduced, usually after the car has slowed down because centrifugal forces and body roll have reduced as a consequence of less momentum.

The same scenario applies for a standing start which will result in one wheel spinning excessively, and the other produces wheelspin to a lesser degree. Apart from a loss in acceleration, the diff doesn't take kindly to being excessively wheelspun, and can fail completely.

The solution to these problems is to replace the standard open differential with a limited slip differential. Limited slip differentials (LSDs) can be classified into two distinct types: those that operate by sensing load, sometimes known as torque sensing (Torsen) and those that operate by sensing speed. A third alternative which performs a similar task to a limited slip diff is a viscous coupling.

LIMITED SLIP TYPES

Depending on what car you have,

an LSD might already be fitted as either original equipment (OE) by the manufacturer, or by a previous owner. Even if your car does have an OE fit LSD, it may still be possible to swap it for a different type or different model depending on your preference and, perhaps, the use to which you put the car. For those cars equipped with an open differential you will have to check what is available for your make and model.

Dealing with load sensing types first, the most common after market fitting will be the Quaife, and as an OE fit the Torsen - as first seen in the original Audi Quattro in the 80s and still used in Audis and other performance road cars today. Of the speed sensing types, these will be clutch pack or plate types. As after market options for road cars, there is generally a choice between the Trannex or Gripper, more recently Jack Knight and, no longer available new, the Salisbury Power-Lok. Original equipment clutch plate types for road cars are most likely to be ZF fitted to some BMWs and, going back a few years, the top spec Ford Capris. Other diffs you hear less of are the cam and pawl (ZF or Jack Knight) and the AP Suretrak, and we'll look at those as well.

If you are planning on foraging for an OE fit diff in a car breakers yard, bear in mind that quite often a higher specification model from the manufacturer of your car will have an original equipment LSD that you can fit to your car (e.g. Sierra 4x4, TVR, etc). Make sure you know what type of LSD it is, i.e. load sensing or speed sensing, as well as knowing the brand name because brand names can be misleading. Also, note that several manufacturers have used a variety of different LSDs in their models over the years, not just switching makes but function type as well, BMW, for instance, has used ZFs clutch packs and Torsens gears (the latter in the Z3). A point to check when buying second-hand, is that if the final drive ratio isn't the one you need then your existing crownwheel and pinion will have to be swapped, and setting the backlash is an expert job.

TORQUE SENSING (TORSEN)

As mentioned earlier, one of the most widely available after market torque sensing type of LSD is the Automatic Torque Biasing (ATB) Quaife. It consists of floating, helically cut gear pinions meshing with sun gears which produce a progressive limiting action which is free on wheel overrun and never fully locks. This type is slightly more expensive than some others, but if you plan to keep your car for many years or drive high mileage, in the long term, it should represent the best value for money. It is also probably the most suitable type for a fast road car. In use with a full throttle standing start, a Quaife locks almost instantly, which, in rear wheel drive cars produces a

quick flick out of the rear end which needs correction with opposite lock. Mid-corner the action also locks but not solid, across both wheels, so no forward momentum is lost except where a driven wheel lifts (likewise for the Torsen, except for the very latest ones which have built in pre load). The reason for this is that the Quaife requires residual torque and, with a driven wheel in the air, it doesn't get any. Momentum is lost until the airborne wheel lowers providing residual torque again. Of course, if your car doesn't lift a driven wheel, this simply doesn't matter. With a Quaife in a front wheel drive car on a standing start you need only a finger light touch on the steering wheel and the car simply pulls forwards in a straight line. In other driving conditions there will be less understeer compared with a clutch pack plate diff. Quaife aside, Torsen has an after market performance range, but this is primarily aimed at the US market. A final point on torsen diffs, whether the original or the ATB from Quaife, is that because they work by a system of gears and not clutch plates

they are not truly limiting slip diffs and are not 'slippers' but 'whirly gears'.

CLUTCH PACK/PLATE

The most common type of speed sensing (or non-Torsen) LSDs is the clutch plate type - a true 'slipper' or 'slippery' differential. ZF calls its the 'Multiple Disc Self Locking', and this type of diff consists of the normal sun and planet gear arrangement like an open diff but is, crucially, stronger in having a greater number of pinion pins and planet gears instead of just the regular 1 pin and 2 gears. The limiting action is achieved by an integral design of a series of clutch type plates. The ZF, Gripper, and Trannex have a 2 pin 4 gear design, but the Xtrac Salisbury type has a 3 gear design. When the differential is in use, these plates lock or release according to the loading on the differential in conjunction with pre-set friction limits. The limiting action of the plates allows drive to be transferred to the non-spinning wheel. This type of differential is likely to have a higher wear rate than a Quaife or other Torsen type of diff, and will need

A cutaway of the Quaife ATB (Automatic Torque Biasing) diff.

A closer look at the inside of a typical clutch plate type diff.

periodic re-building with replacement plates, whether an OE diff from ZF or a TranX. A key difference between a clutch plate diff and the torsen is that it doesn't have a locking action such that both wheels have near equal power transmitted to them but switches power to the wheel with most or all the grip. The ratio of the slip can vary according to what you ask for, but typically might be 30-70 per cent. So, with one driven wheel fully airborne, the other wheel is still fed up to 70 per cent of the available power and, mid-corner, almost full momentum is maintained, unless, of course, you break a halfshaft or driveshaft. From a full throttle standing start with a clutch pack/plate diff, acceleration is much more rapid than with an open diff, and wheelspin is possible which produces a dramatic but stable fish-tailing or snaking action in a rear wheel drive car that shouldn't be corrected - let the diff sort itself, point the front wheels straight ahead, and feather back on the throttle till grip is regained. On a front wheel drive car, the car can weave from side to side slightly on full throttle starts.

A final point on slipper diffs is that they can be tuned to suit your driving style and your car, at the point of manufacturing or rebuild, particularly the latter, with significant differences in the settings between front wheel drive and rear wheel drive cars.

CAM & PAWL

The cam and pawl type of LSD was invented in the 1930s and first produced by ZF. More recently other manufacturers made cam and pawl LSDs, including a range made by Jack Knight. The cam and pawl is better suited to the race track by virtue of its maintenance needs and wear characteristics, and is not recommended for a road car. Further, some users have described it as 'ratchety' and harsh. It's a relatively rare diff, and was generally much more expensive than other LSDs; I haven't found any recent model listing for the diff and expect there will be little or nothing available for modern cars.

AP SURETRAC

A newer type of LSD is the Suretrac Torsen from AP, but that only marketed for a short time and hasn't, at the time of publishing, been available in Britain for about two years. This diff delivers the greatest torque to the tyre, with the best grip before wheelspin occurs. It was available for use with 2.3, 2.8, and 3.1 final drive ratios, predominantly on Peugeot cars, but also on the MGF and Volkswagen Golf to name but two. I haven't driven a Suretrac driven car, so can't comment on its driving characteristics. The unit itself was sealed for life and not designed to be rebuilt, and, while no longer available here, Fuji in Japan makes some, although these units are sometimes used in the rear of an Impreza. If your car has a Suretrac and it's worn out, and unless you have an Impreza, you'll need to buy something completely different to replace it.

WELDED DIFFS & SPOOLS

If you really are on a budget, or happen to be a drag racer, you can do without a diff action altogether and weld up the sun and planet gears to get what is perhaps not surprisingly known as a 'welded' diff. A neater alternative is to have the same thing made (known as a spool) which, by virtue of design, will be a lot lighter. The welded diff

AP Suretrak cutaway and complete diff side-by-side. (Courtesy - AP Racing)

A stripped down Ferguson viscous coupling. (Courtesy - FFD Ricardo)

or spool is 100 per cent locked all the time and, from a standing start, drives like a Torsen or Quaife, only more so, but mid-corner is closer to a slipper. If you have to drive it slowly around town, it will be unpleasant, noisy, and jumpy, because one wheel will be snatching and scrubbing all the way through a corner, especially a tight one. It's included here for reference and in case your fast road car has one fitted. If it was something you have contemplated as a solution - it's not!

VISCOUS COUPLINGS (VC FERGUSON)

These were invented in 1969 and used ever since, especially on 4WD and FWD cars such as Lancias, the original and scarcely seen Jensen FF, as well as some very specialised rally, touring car and Indy cars. A Ferguson viscous coupling (VC) is usually placed between one driveshaft and a driven wheel; as grip is lost at one wheel due to wheelspin, the coupling provides increasing resistance and ensures drive is transferred to the other wheel. On 4WD cars, a viscous coupling is sometimes used instead of a central differential, to control the amount of driving force (torque) transmitted to either the front or rear wheels, depending on which has the most

available grip. I'm not aware of any after market conversions to viscous couplings but if you know different please let me know.

PHANTOM GRIP

Something relatively new in the diff world, that originated in the USA and is just breaking ground here in the UK, is the Phantom Grip which achieves a very similar result to an LSD but for a fraction of the price. There is no catch, but with all things you get what you pay for and, while with a true LSD you purchase a completely new diff with the limited action, with this new product you keep your old diff, adding the parts to change the nature of the way it works. The product is called Phantom Grip and, when fitted to any conventional open diff, converts it to a limited slip action.

The Phantom Grip unit itself is sprung, and two spring ratings are available - gold for street use and green for competition or more aggressive use. Also included with the unit and the alternative springs are comprehensive illustrated fitting instructions, that assume that the diff you are going

to use is in good condition. Because the Phantom Grip modifies your car's existing open differential, it is required to be removed from the car for conversion - be sure to have the necessary gaskets, tools (including a torque wrench), and confidence to undertake the job yourself before proceeding.

A typical installation of the Phantom Grip will require partial dismantling of the differential since the unit is installed with the diff cross pin running through its centre, with each side positioned to work against the sun gears. The sun gears benefit from the rough surface facing being smoothed off with emery paper to aid the breaking in process of the Phantom grip, otherwise the differential can be reassembled and re-fitted. However, given that unlike fitting the Phantom Grip uses all of the existing differential parts, you might want to give consideration to having the differential overhauled at the same time.

In use, and from a standing start, the action falls somewhere between an open diff and the Quaife, which, in practice, means it is progressive

The Phantom Grip unit.

The Phantom Grip unit installed in a conventional open diff.

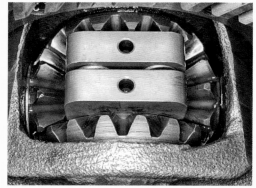

in action but very driver friendly. When cornering, where grip levels are exceeded, the unit is again very driver friendly, allowing a steady 4 wheel drift to be maintained and the car driven and steered on the throttle. In summary, you get what you pay for and, while I am not claiming this product is a match for a pure limited slip diff, I do believe it is a good budget alternative, and the is available for a wide range of makes of cars, including: Honda, Porsche, Mazda, Toyota, and VW.

MAKE YOUR SELECTION - WHICH TYPE OF DIFF TO CHOOSE & WHY

Assuming that you do have more than one type of diff action to choose from, your decision for selection needs to be based on the type of driving you are going to do, the type and weight of your car, and how much you can afford and how often, e.g. for rebuilds. Generally, a load sensing diff like an ATB Quaife is more suited to road use than a clutch pack/plate because it will wear well and is reliable, but is held to be less effective than speed sensing types if the car will be cornered on 3 wheels (i.e. on the racetrack). That said, a lightweight but powerful car with a high degree of roll stiffness may lift a wheel on the public highway.

There is no such drawback with the speed sensing diffs that are available but, because the plates can wear very quickly, even with very regular diff oil changes, they can work out very expensive in the long run. If you bear those two factors in mind and base your decision accordingly you should get value for money. The welded diff is cheapest of all but with the most drawbacks, and for track use only. Next, is the other budget option - the Phantom Grip which is road user friendly, the least expensive, but ultimately not as strong as true LSDs. Last, but not least, is the viscous coupling which is something not generally available as an after market option. However, it may be possible to transplant one from a higher or sporting specification model similar to your own car, assuming you have a base model. In short, it is simple but effective.

DIFF CARRIER

Some older cars, particularly Fords, use a cast iron differential carrier or housing. If your car has a cast iron differential carrier, it is worth the money to have it replaced with an aluminium alloy item, bearing in mind it's not just a weight saving but an unsprung weight saving; Burton Power can sell you one.

Diff carrier assembly mounted in live axle (shown on axle stands).

Alloy diff carrier from Burton Power to replace the cast iron item on Ford English axle. (Courtesy - Burton Power)

Chapter 12
Brakes

INTRODUCTION

Improvements to the braking system of your vehicle will primarily improve the deceleration (braking) of your vehicle. Additionally, acceleration and handling can improve if the weight of the braking components is reduced. Because the braking components comprise unsprung weight, the advantage in reducing weight is greater than would at first appear.

Warning! - Braking might well appear an uninteresting part of your vehicle's performance, however, when building a fast car for the road, it is more important that it will stop fast than accelerate fast. The brakes on your car are what makes it stop, which seems a pretty obvious statement to make; think what you are taking for granted, though, and then give some thought to the demands you place on brakes and what they have to do. The key principle when thinking about brakes is that they do the opposite to the engine in that they decelerate

the car. The more power the car's engine develops to accelerate the car, the harder the car's brakes have to work to decelerate it. In terms of overall performance, as a car's rate of acceleration is determined by its power to weight ratio, so braking performance is similarly determined. With brakes, however, the rate of deceleration is determined by the ratio of weight to braking power (torque). A further consideration is that the brakes need to be consistent in delivering the braking torque, in other words, they continue to work just as well when being worked hard and often.

Given that a car's braking performance is determined by its braking-power-to-weight ratio then two types of change to the car will stop it quicker. The first is more braking power and the second is less weight. Note that second point about weight because, although no one usually fits less powerful brakes on a car, owners often put more weight into it, which

is as likely to be in car entertainment equipment in the boot (trunk).

Another aspect of braking is that, just as a more powerful engine will require more cooling, so more braking power will require more cooling. The harder the brakes work, the more heat is generated. Sometimes, the only reason more powerful brakes are fitted is that they are easier to cool by virtue of their design, but more of that later. However, the most efficient solution is to use the smallest brakes, and thereby lightest, that will get the job done with a safety margin.

Another factor in braking performance also bears comparison to acceleration and that is grip, or lack of it. Just as excessive power can cause the tyres to lose grip, with resultant wheelspin and loss of acceleration, so the reverse is true of excessive braking power. Once the wheels are locked and the tyres are skidding, deceleration is largely lost. Put another way - you need to match braking power to grip. An increase in grip can shorten the braking distance if the braking system can utilise that grip. Even if the braking system is fitted with an anti-lock system, if the grip is increased the stopping distance will still be shortened, again subject to the car utilising that grip.

All of the above factors make it quite hard to plan what the braking upgrades need to be. However, following each section of this chapter in order will prevent unnecessary expenditure. To help you make the choices consult the following menu:

TOP SIX OPTIONS FOR IMPROVING BRAKING PERFORMANCE

1. Replace brake fluid with new fluid of DOT 5.1 rating.
2. Replace all flexible brake hoses with braided steel hoses.
3. Replace friction material (pads and shoes) with high performance material.
4. Fit larger front discs, vented and grooved if possible.
5. Fit larger and lighter brake calipers.
6. Replace rear drums with discs or grooved type brake drums, as applicable.

BRAKE FLUID

The brake fluid used in your car's braking system is very important and therefore merits consideration before the rest of the braking system. The best braking system money can buy will perform poorly if the brake fluid is not appropriate to the task. A modified road car that is more demanding than a standard car will require a better brake fluid than that normally specified. This is because, as the brake components dissipate heat when in use, some of that heat is passed to the brake fluid. When the temperature of the fluid reaches its boiling point it vaporises. This vapour is compressible,

resulting in a depressed brake pedal compressing vapour instead of displacing fluid, the net effect being no, or poor, brakes. The solution is to use an appropriate fluid of one of three main categories: mineral, silicone or polyglycol-based.

You are only likely to find mineral fluid in Citroens and Rolls-Royces. If your vehicle is one of these makes and is using mineral fluid you must not use anything else and must be particularly careful about any changes made to the braking system, checking with the parts supplier of any nonstandard hydraulics parts, before fitting, to establish that they will work both safely and satisfactorily with mineral fluid.

For all other cars either silicone, or more conventionally polyglycol, fluid is used. The principal difference between silicone and polyglycol fluid is that the former is not hygroscopic (it does not absorb moisture from the atmosphere). Silicone brake fluid will preserve the interior of hydraulic pipes, it also has a long service life, but is expensive and is not suitable for most high performance applications. The reason it is not suitable is that it becomes compressible at high temperatures and does not have a 'dry' boiling point as high as high performance polyglycol fluids. Silicone fluid may not be hygroscopic, but if any moisture or water is present in the system it remains 'free' water and can produce vapour lock at temperatures as low as 100C (212F). Also, when changing from polyglycol to silicone fluid, or vice versa, you'll need to thoroughly clean the system and possibly renew the pipes and seals, though not everyone agrees on this point.

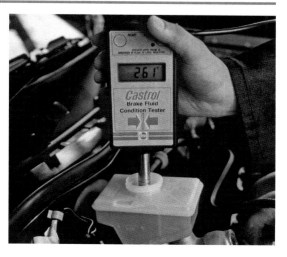

Brake fluid needs a high boiling point to work effectively and can be tested by using a Castrol brake fluid tester. The biggest improvement you can make to the brakes is to replace old/low boiling point fluid with fresh brake fluid. (Courtesy - Castrol)

The reason being that although silicone and polyglycol fluid are compatible they are not miscible (they will not mix). I have heard of problems with brake seals when silicone fluid has been used, especially on older cars.

All fluids are graded in relation to the way they are affected by temperature. There are four common standards which are: DOT 3 (J1703); DOT 4; DOT 5 (silicone) and DOT 5.1. I have omitted the DOT 5 values in the accompanying table. The DOT value relates to the wet and dry boiling points of the fluid. The dry boiling point is measured using fresh fluid. The wet boiling point is measured after the

	DOT 3	DOT 4	DOT 5
Dry	205C 401F	230C 446F	268C 514F
Wet	140C 284F	155C 311F	191C 375F

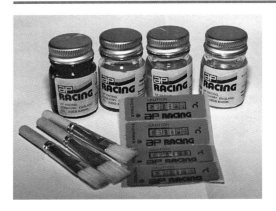

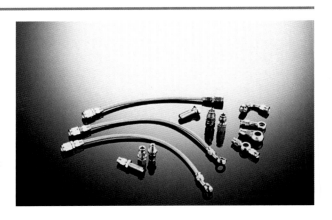

The sure way to establish whether the brakes are operating within their working range is to use the AP Racing heat sensitive paint kit. (Courtesy - AP Racing)

A braided steel hose brake line kit from Rally Design. (Courtesy - Rally Design)

fluid has been exposed to a controlled humidity and has, therefore, absorbed some moisture. The respective dry and wet boiling points for DOT 3, DOT 4, and DOT 5.1 are as shown in the accompanying chart: a higher DOT number equates to higher dry and wet boiling points. The 'dry' standard is the important one because frequent change of fluid means the fluid never comes close to being classed as 'wet'. **Warning!** - Fluid must be changed every twelve months, or less, for high performance applications, and monthly if you use your car in motorsports and use non-race brake fluid. Generally, Castrol DOT 4 fluid will give good results, and AP's DOT 5.1 fluid will give equally good if not better results (by virtue of its rating). **Warning!** - Cheap fluids and any brand of DOT 3 fluid are not worth considering for a fast road car because of their inferior performance. **Warning!** - Don't be tempted to use a race-type brake fluid in a road car because of its comparatively low wet boiling point. Put another way, a race fluid absorbs moisture much more quickly than a normal fluid.

BRAKE HOSES
The standard brake hoses can be replaced by metal braided hoses such as Goodridge stainless steel hoses. The fittings for the hoses may be of steel or

anodised aluminium alloy. Using this type of hose results in a much firmer brake pedal that not only provides better braking 'feel,' but a faster action on initial application. It is possible to buy an off-the-shelf braided hose kit for most popular cars. If, however, you can't find an off-the-shelf kit, it is not much more expensive to have the hoses custom made. If you are using nonstandard calipers on your car, you may need to have hoses made specially anyway. **Warning!** - Whatever hoses you use, and especially when brakes, wheels, and suspension components have been modified, make sure there is no contact between the hoses and anything else through full suspension articulation and full front wheel steering movement. If there is contact you must re-route the pipe or use a different length of pipe to remove the problem.

FRICTION MATERIALS
Brake friction materials, sometimes known as brake linings, are the materials bonded or riveted onto the metal part of a brake pad or shoe. The friction material makes contact with the brake disc or drum friction surface when the brake pedal is pressed. This contact creates friction which ultimately slows the car down. The friction in turn creates heat, and it is this heat that can cause problems. The harder the brakes

are used, either because of the speed or weight of the vehicle or the level of deceleration being attempted, the greater the heat developed. For a fast road car that has been power tuned, the standard brake friction material may not have a sufficiently high heat rating to cope with the deceleration asked of it. There are two solutions: one is to improve heat dissipation of the brakes by fitting larger or more effective components, such as grooved and vented (ventilated) discs; the second is to fit a friction material that has a higher heat rating. In some instances, the only choice will be to choose the latter and, in others, the problem may be such that both approaches will need to be adopted: however, this section is only dealing with friction material. **Warning!** - The key point is that the use of too high a temperature range friction material will result in glazing of the pad surface, and poor, if not dangerous, braking performance (such a material simply will not work well at the relatively low temperatures generated by normal road use). Put another way, do not be tempted to use racing friction material on a road car in the mistaken belief that the brakes will work better. The reason for this is that any friction material has an effective working heat range that includes a lower limit as well as an upper one.

Overkill even for a track and fast road car, – a 6 pot (piston) caliper from AP Racing. Instead of trying to use it, take a look at the excellent range of 4 pot (piston) calipers the company produces.

from a reputable supplier such as Mintex.

GENERAL PRINCIPLES OF HYDRAULICS

If you are contemplating any change to the hydraulic components of your car, bear in mind the basic principle of an hydraulic system. The pressure put into the system (i.e. depression of the brake pedal) will produce an equal pressure everywhere in the system. However, the equal pressure exerted elsewhere is proportional to the area in which it is applied. As an example, a system pressure of 1000psi would produce 1000lb of pressure on a one square inch piston, but only 500lb on a piston half the size. That same 1000psi on two square inch pistons would produce 2000lb. What this means when you are modifying the brakes is that if you increase the size of the slave end of the braking system, i.e. brake caliper piston area by size (or quantity) or drum slave cylinder piston area, you will end up with more brake travel than you had originally because more fluid is required to fill the bigger voids left by the displaced pistons.

Alternatively, if you change the master cylinder size you achieve the same effect in reverse. For instance, if you find that the new pedal travel is excessive then to restore the status quo of the system you will need to fit a larger master cylinder. However, if you replace a single master cylinder with twin cylinders, increasing master cylinder area may be unavoidable and you will increase brake pedal loadings. The only way to reduce them back to something more manageable will be

GENERAL PRINCIPLES OF HYDRAULICS

Change	Effect	Solution
Increase in slave piston area because of larger piston size or number	Longer brake pedal travel, softer pedal	Increase master cylinder size
Increase in master cylinder size because of larger piston size or number	Shorter brake pedal travel, harder pedal	Fit brake servo or increase servo size
Reduction in slave piston area	Shorter brake pedal travel & harder pedal	Fit brake servo or increase servo size
Reduction in master cylinder size (in isolation of any other change	Longer brake pedal travel	Don't reduce master cylinder size

With racing friction material, although the upper limit is higher than road material so is the lower limit and when working outside its working range it is ineffective. Simply, racing material doesn't work when cold. The solution is to buy a high performance friction material that is suitable for road use

by fitting a brake servo, or if your car already has one, fitting a larger one or even twin units.

The braking system input pressure is derived from the pedal effort exerted by your foot multiplied by the leverage ratio of the pedal.

PEDALS

There are not many instances where you might want to change to a different brake pedal. However, if you do, note that not all pedals have the same leverage ratio. The range is normally from about 3:1 up to 5:1. If you assume an applied pedal pressure of 100lb, you'll have hydraulic input of 300lb or 500lb depending on the pedal ratio, so the leverage ratio does make a big difference. What one person considers a 'firm' pedal another may consider 'soft.' However, 100lb appears to be an agreeable figure, with less needed for servoed brakes. In any event, maximum required pedal

pressure should not exceed 300lb for a man and 200lb for a woman. I mention these figures because they may be useful if you are calculating what size of servo may be required.

MASTER CYLINDERS

Most modern production cars have a combined master cylinder/servo unit that is not easily replaced. If you are fitting a nonstandard brake master cylinder(s) however, perhaps to solve an engine bay clearance problem, take a look at the range from AP Racing and read the section below on servos. Also note that quite often the fluid reservoir can be sited remote from the cylinder. Be careful about sizing the cylinder and seek expert advice if in any doubt.

SERVOS, INCLUDING REMOTE TYPES

The brake servo is sometimes known as a 'power booster', which is a better

description because that is what it does. However, what gets boosted is the power of your right leg rather than the hydraulic pressure exerted. As mentioned in the master cylinder section, most modern production cars have a servo built into the brake master cylinder assembly. Turning to the rating of the servo itself, if you assume a typical manifold vacuum versus atmospheric pressure across the diaphragm giving an applied pressure of ten psi, and then multiply it by the area of the diaphragm, you get the value of pressure assistance. The size of the diaphragm is usually expressed as a diameter, such as ten inches (645mm), rather than an area. To calculate the area, first halve the diameter to get the radius and then multiply the radius squared by pi. Note that if a nonstandard carburettor, or fuel injection manifold, is used, it might be the case that the servo draws on vacuum from one inlet rather than all the engine inlets and this can affect its efficiency to a degree.

Given that a larger servo will not improve braking efficiency by itself, there would not appear to be a good reason to change it. However, if you want to change to a different brake master cylinder, perhaps to fit a twin master cylinder setup, you may need to fit a different combined master/servo unit or fit a remote servo to restore acceptable pedal pressure.

An engine swap, for instance, might place a demand on space in the engine bay. It might even be the case that the servo cannot be sited in its original location and, perhaps, not in the engine bay at all. If this is the case, then it is important to size both the master cylinder and servo correctly. Refer to the accompanying General Principles of Hydraulics table if you have made other braking system changes which will have a

An upgrade kit from Brembo. (Courtesy - Brembo)

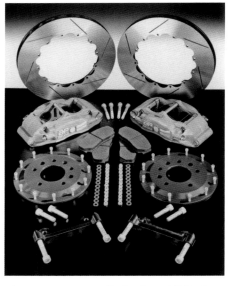

A remote master cylinder from AP Racing. (Courtesy - AP Racing)

Everything you'll ever need in a brake conversion kit. (Courtesy - AP Racing)

bearing on the size of the components you select. The choice of remote servos is somewhat limited, though a brake specialist can sometimes source something that was fitted to an older car from the days when it was common for cars to have a remote servo. Finally, it is, of course, possible to do away with the servo altogether - if you can live with the pedal pressure then required.

BRAKE BIAS ADJUSTMENT

Because of the weight transfer from the rear to the front of the car during braking, most modern cars have a limiting valve to ensure that the front brakes lock a fraction before those at the rear. With anti-lock braking systems (such as ABS) this is all taken care of by the system. **Warning!** - Modifications to the braking system can cause problems with anti-lock systems, so seek expert advice before modifying cars so equipped.

Where a limiting valve is fitted, it will, in most cases, be unable to respond to improvements you make to the braking system, weight or balance of the car. So, if you have considerably lightened the car, or even increased the weight of it, you may find you have a braking balance problem. For instance, consider a typical iron block, front engine, rear wheel drive car. The standard engine is replaced by an alloy Rover V8 that sits further back in the car, and the boot (trunk) is full of a serious sound system (ICE). The weight, and weight bias, of the car will have changed considerably - a recipe for brake bias problems. Luckily, on many cars, the front brakes are usually sufficiently larger than the rears for things not to get out of hand. However, if you want spot-on brakes, you'll need to adjust the brake bias. The easiest and best way to do

Remote servo kit from AP Racing.

this is by fitting an adjustable bias (or proportioning) valve. Once you have the valve installed all that remains is for it to be set to suit the changed weight bias of the car.

The alternative method that allows brake bias adjustment front to rear is the fitting of twin master cylinders in conjunction with a balance bar. This type of installation is a lot more involved, and more expensive, than using a bias valve. If a proprietary kit is available then use it, if not, you'll need to build something from scratch.

LINE LOCKS

A 'line lock' is a piece of equipment that, when plumbed into the brake hydraulic system, allows the front brakes to be isolated from those at the rear and, in effect, allows the use of two wheel braking.

There are two situations for which you might want this facility (but not on the public highway). The first is for a rear wheel drive car so that you can switch all the braking force to the front wheels, put one foot on the brake pedal to lock them and the other foot hard on the throttle and perform a drag racing-type burnout with the car remaining stationary. The switch is not prohibitively expensive in relation to the tyres!

The RML Micra sporting big Brembo drilled discs and Brembo calipers.

The second situation is where all the braking force is switched to the rear wheels. The foot brake can then be used to lock the rear wheels in isolation, giving much the same effect as using the handbrake to perform handbrake turns.

If you plan to fit a line lock, you'll need to look at the schematic for the braking lines on your car to ensure that they are suitable. If the system has dual circuit brakes it may not be possible to fit the line lock and get it to work. It may also be the case that your local laws prohibit the fitting of such a device to a road car.

BRAKE DISCS

It is the disc size that ultimately limits how much energy can be absorbed by the braking system. However, disc size is limited by the size of wheels used on the vehicle. For a vehicle with thirteen inch diameter wheels the choices are very limited, but if your chosen vehicle uses fourteen inch or larger diameter wheels, or can be modified to take them, then the choice is wider.

The disc is the key to braking performance. Disc diameter is important because the further the calipers are from the centre of the wheel, the greater the leverage ratio applied to their action (force x distance applies). Also, because braking friction produces heat, which the disc has to absorb and disperse, the larger the disc the larger the physical mass of metal (ignoring carbon discs) and the greater the heat

energy that can be absorbed for any given temperature rise. It can be seen that the thickness as well as the diameter of the disc has a part to play here, though the thickness is secondary because an increase in thickness, and therefore mass, aids heat absorption but does nothing for dissipation (which an increase in disc diameter does). Because dispersion of heat is so important to disc design, some disks are vented (ventilated) to aid cooling. Sometimes a vented disc is, in fact, made from two halves, and in other cases it is one piece. A problem with early designs of vented discs is that they had a tendency to warp when overheated - something to be avoided. **Warning!** - The design of the vanes in a vented disc can be such that they are handed from one side of the car to the other (i.e. each is designed for use on only one side of the car), and this is a point to watch when fitting vented discs for the first time.

Some discs, whether vented or not, have grooves in the friction faces. The grooves are designed to aid the release of hot gases generated during braking and to increase surface area for cooling purposes. Some discs are drilled to aid brake cooling and, although it is possible to have a set of discs drilled after purchase, this modification has been known to lead to problems.

ROAD AND RACE CALIPERS

There are three main differences between road and race calipers, though, as will be explained later, this distinction is more blurred than it used to be. The differences are as follows: race calipers are much more expensive; they are made from aluminium alloy, sometimes with titanium pistons, and are, therefore, lighter (road calipers are usually cast iron with steel pistons); they don't have dirt/dust seals.

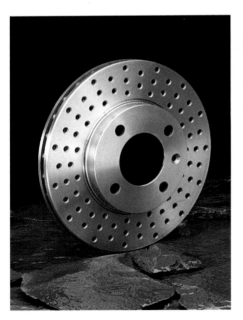

**Drilled and vented disc from Tarox.
(Courtesy - GGB (Engineering Spares) Ltd.)**

Drilled and vented disc.

**Grooved and vented disc from Tarox.
(Courtesy - GGB (Engineering Spares) Ltd.)**

Twin piston lightweight caliper from AP Racing. (Courtesy - AP Racing)

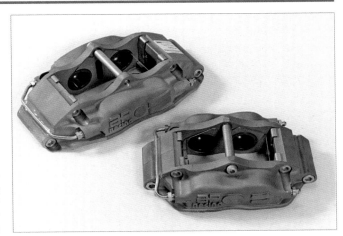

Two different sizes of four piston lightweight calipers from AP Racing. (Courtesy - AP Racing)

However, it is no longer the case that aluminium calipers are exclusive to racing cars. AP Racing, and others to a lesser extent, have produced a range of affordable aluminium calipers for road use which, while not quite as light as out-and-out race calipers, are still considerably lighter than cast iron calipers. The weight advantage is very useful but, that aside, because the calipers come in a range of sizes it is relatively easy to upgrade both disc and caliper for a whole variety of cars.

The AP Racing road calipers also have the all important dirt/dust seals. Racing calipers do without these seals because the calipers used on a race car are stripped, cleaned, and reassembled on a frequent basis. Also, their usage, though hard, is limited to track conditions that are clean in comparison to the public highway. Ingress of dirt is, therefore, not a major problem, and those regular rebuilds ensure even slight piston or cylinder wear is remedied. On a road car the reverse conditions apply and, therefore, racing calipers should only be used with caution, and this should be borne in mind when making your purchase.

The size of the caliper is important because an overly ambitious choice, especially in relation to the disc size,

whether or not standard size discs are used, can lead to wheel clearance problems. The other consideration is that a larger caliper will weigh more and increase unsprung weight, though switching to an aluminium caliper redresses this problem somewhat, if not completely.

REAR DRUM TO DISC CONVERSIONS

If the rear axle of your car is fitted with drum brakes then, in the vast majority of cases, you are stuck with them. The reason for this is that although it is relatively straightforward to fit discs and calipers in place of drums, as is the case with many racing cars and modern road cars, a road car must have a handbrake. So, fitting a small disc and caliper setup to the rear axle of your car may infringe legislative requirements unless a handbrake system is built in. If a similar but more powerful model of your car is fitted with discs, as opposed to your car's drums, it may be possible to do a conversion. Likewise, for a few cars, suitable rear disc conversions do exist. However, if you are stuck with drums, there are a few things you can do to improve the performance.

Drum brake modifications

For some models - the Mini is a good example - it is possible to replace the standard cast iron drums with aluminium alloy items. The advantage is in the reduction in the overall weight of the car and the unsprung weight in particular.

Much more widely available than aluminium alloy drums are Tarox drums with grooves machined into the braking surface. The grooves allow hot gas and brake dust to be released and increase surface area for cooling purposes, and this permits the brake shoes to operate at maximum efficiency. However, if you have done the brake testing recommended later in this chapter you may find that the car actually doesn't need any more braking force at the rear (assuming the vehicle is disc/drum - front/rear) so such a modification would not be necessary.

BRAKE DYNO TESTING & ROAD TESTING

After each modification to the braking system on your car you should do a static check. For this you will need to have the engine running to provide a vacuum for the servo and, with the car stationary, press the brake pedal and hold it down. What you are checking is that the pedal is not only firm but stays firm and doesn't sink. If the pedal is spongy there is air in the system that will need to be bled out. If the pedal slowly sinks there is a fluid leak that must be stopped. **Warning!** - Under no circumstances drive the car until the problem is fixed. If the static check is satisfactory, a low speed (15mph) emergency stop can be undertaken. If the car pulls to one side, check that the brakes on the opposite side of the car are working properly and that they are not seized.

If the low speed check is satisfactory the car should be driven to a vehicle testing station and the brakes checked on the roller brake tester. The braking torque figures should be noted and any problems rectified. The final check can only be undertaken at a reasonable speed and therefore, for safety reasons, done on a private road - perhaps a large empty car park (parking lot). Emergency stops are undertaken such that the wheels lock. **Warning!** - The front wheels need to lock first. If the rears lock first a tail slide will follow, leading to a spin. This problem is most easily rectified by fitting a brake bias valve,

BRAKING DISTANCES

On a good dry road an average vehicle should be able to stop in the distances detailed in the accompanying table, a fast road car in less. On a wet road you could probably double the distances.

Speed (mph) ft/second	Speed in distance (ft)	Braking
30	44	45
45	66	101
60	88	180
70	102	245
90	132	405
100	147	500
120	176	720
130	191	845
140	205	980

One mile = 5280 feet
60mph = one mile a minute or 5280 feet per minute or 88 feet per second.

and adjusting the front to rear setting. An alternative approach would be to increase the size/power of the front brakes or reduce the size/power of the rear brakes. Once all that has been done it is possible to measure stopping distances from 60mph to zero using a G Tech performance meter from Autocar Electrical.

Drums, of which this is a typical example, will appear at the rear only, other than on very old cars.

Chapter 13

Suspension - general

INTRODUCTION

Changes to a car's suspension will affect the cornering speed aspect of performance. However, to a lesser extent, the other three aspects of performance may also be affected. Acceleration and deceleration both cause a weight transfer to take place and the suspension plays a part in limiting these effects. Straight line top speed may be improved because a reduction in ride height has reduced the coefficient of drag.

The general principles and general advice on suspension are contained in this chapter; subsequent chapters deal with anything specific to front or rear suspension. Although the means of achieving suspension modifications vary in relation to the type of suspension the car being modified has, the general principles are the same for all types of system.

To get the best from your modifications you need to first put the car through a total alignment check to

find out what state it is in. For instance, are components old and worn, possibly even damaged, or poorly set up? Once you have a clear starting point you can plan, cost and then carry out the modifications in a logical sequence as suggested by the 'Order of Decision' table. You may, however, still want to evaluate the effect each

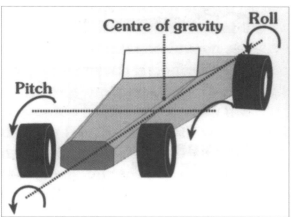

The principle dynamic forces acting upon a car are roll and pitch.

change has had before undertaking another. Part of that evaluation will also require you to have at least a rudimentary understanding of what the suspension does, why it does it, and terminology. Useful advice on how to solve or reduce undesirable effects can be found in the 'Solving Handling Problems' panel, but first the basics.

UNDERSTEER & OVERSTEER

Whenever a car turns its tyres create a sideways or cornering force. This results in the tyre running with a 'slip angle' (the angle between the direction in which it is pointing and the direction in which it is being forced to travel by the inertia of the car to which it is attached). The front and rear tyres rarely run at the same angle when the car is cornering. When the front tyres run the greatest slip angle the effect is known as 'understeer', and is usually felt by the driver as the front end of the car wanting to run slightly wide of the cornering line. If the rear slip angle is the greater, the condition is known as 'oversteer'. The driver usually feels the rear end of the car wanting to run slightly wide of the corner.

Very generally speaking, a front wheel drive car will tend to understeer and a rear wheel drive car will tend to oversteer. If you want to know what the difference feels like in practice, go for a drive in a front wheel drive car and then, straight afterwards, a rear wheel drive car, or vice versa.

There is a lot of talk about whether it is better to have understeer or oversteer, the truth is that it is better to have neither. A neutral handling car, in our case from tuned suspension, is the ideal to aim for. Note, as well, that the generalisations about understeer and oversteer are just that. It's possible to have a car that will have slight understeering properties when cornering hard, but cornering harder will produce a sudden and large amount of oversteer. That sounds awful, but in practice the handling may be predictable and is perfectly safe. **Warning!** - Note that predictable handling, rather than precise but nervous handling is preferable, but it is your car and your choice.

ROLL

As a vehicle is cornered, there is an outward weight transfer which the car body reacts to by rolling about its central axis. The amount of roll is dependant on many things, including the height of the vehicle (more specifically the centre of gravity), the weight of the vehicle, its resistance to roll (a feature of suspension), the amount of grip, and the speed the

corner is being taken at. However, the greater the roll the greater the reduction in grip at the wheels due to camber changes induced by the roll. Put another way, as roll increases, the tyre contact patch loses effectiveness and so the car is less

likely to respond to steering input and proceed in the manner intended. Further, the lighter loaded wheels, which will be the ones innermost in relation to the corner, will have little or no useful grip - which may lead to wheelspin. Roll, therefore, is one of the

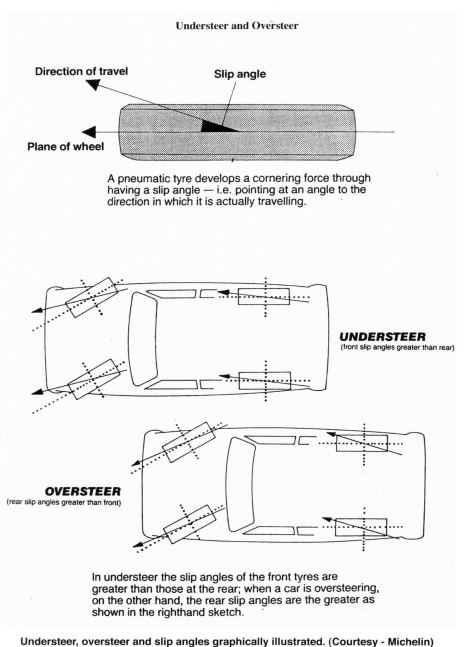

Understeer and Oversteer

Direction of travel

Slip angle

Plane of wheel

A pneumatic tyre develops a cornering force through having a slip angle — i.e. pointing at an angle to the direction in which it is actually travelling.

UNDERSTEER
(front slip angles greater than rear)

OVERSTEER
(rear slip angles greater than front)

In understeer the slip angles of the front tyres are greater than those at the rear; when a car is oversteering, on the other hand, the rear slip angles are the greater as shown in the righthand sketch.

Understeer, oversteer and slip angles graphically illustrated. (Courtesy - Michelin)

greatest enemies of good cornering.

PITCH

As a vehicle accelerates or decelerates there is a weight transfer - either front to rear for acceleration, or vice versa for deceleration. The effect this has is to load or unload the driven wheels (except for 4WD vehicles) and the steering roadwheels. In practice, because increases in load increase grip, it means that a FWD car with a rearward weight transfer under acceleration has less grip at the driven wheels and steered wheels, being therefore likely to lose traction and steering. For a RWD car, the traction will increase under acceleration, but the steering will be less affected than on a FWD car because the front wheels are only being asked to steer and not transfer tractive force as well. All of this explains why purpose-built dragsters are RWD.

COMPLIANCE

Because the vehicle suspension is usually (but with some exceptions) mounted in rubber bushes or other flexible joints, such as track rod end bearings, there is some built-in compliance. When bushings and joints age and wear the compliance can become excessive and lead to sloppiness or vagueness in handling.

DAMPING

When any car spring has a load put into it, for instance under braking, the spring absorbs energy and compresses. Once the load has been released the spring decompresses. A spring, by its very nature, will want to repeat the cycle, a phenomenon known as oscillation, which is undesirable and dangerous in suspension. The spring is prevented from oscillating by the damper (shock absorber), which as its name suggests, damps the action of the spring. Springs and dampers need to be matched, and a change in spring should be accompanied by a change in damper (other than for very minor changes from the original fitment). The reason for matching is that a spring that is overdamped is not allowed to work effectively and the damper overworks leading to premature wear and perhaps fade, the latter a condition in which it overheats and then ceases to function properly. If the damper is too weak for the spring then oscillation can occur. For these reasons it is usually best to purchase springs and dampers as a single package, or purchase adjustable dampers.

CAMBER

Camber is the angle at which the wheel and tyre sit in relation to vertical (in relation to the centre line of the axle). Camber is important because it needs to be right in order to maximise the grip of the tyres, especially at the front. Ideally the camber should be zero. However, because the camber of the front wheels changes as the car rolls, it's desirable to start off with a little negative camber so that, as the car rolls, the wheels are at zero camber and maximum grip is realised from the tyres. Lowering the ride height of the car often changes the static camber setting and, because the lowered ride height of the vehicle causes a reduction in sideways weight transfer, body roll is reduced, so less static negative camber is needed to maximise tyre grip in a turn.

UNSPRUNG WEIGHT

The majority of the car's weight is supported by the car's springs and this is known as 'sprung weight'. The weight of all components not supported by the springs, including the springs themselves, is known as 'unsprung weight'. The unsprung weight, therefore, typically includes: wheels, tyres, brakes, springs, and half the weight of the damper (shock absorber) and suspension links. Note that those parts that connect the vehicle body to the suspension (or form part of it) only count as half weight because one end is part of the sprung weight of the vehicle, while the other end is unsprung. It is possible, and desirable, to reduce unsprung weight by careful suspension design (using such devices as rockers to work with inboard springs and dampers and, therefore, comprise sprung rather than unsprung weight). However, it is beyond the scope of this book to detail how to design and build your own suspension system, but it does, of course, provide advice on how to improve matters with the existing system.

Increasing the ratio of unsprung to sprung weight, especially when it is achieved by reducing the unsprung weight, will improve not only the general handling of the car but also traction (grip) in acceleration and braking, particularly on bumpy road surfaces. The reason for this is that weight creates inertia and the less inertia the unsprung components have, the more easily will the springs keep the tyres in contact with the road. Reducing the vehicle's sprung weight will worsen the ratio, between sprung and unsprung weight, though there are many benefits in reducing overall vehicle weight. Increasing the vehicle weight will improve the ratio, but the benefit will be negated by the poorer handling and general performance. The preferred solution, therefore, is to reduce both unsprung and sprung weight.

TOTAL ALIGNMENT CHECK

A total alignment check involves considerably more than just checking the tracking of your vehicle. Although this type of checking facility is relatively common in the USA, the only company, to my knowledge, to offer it in the UK is Pro-Align in Northampton. The alignment service it offers is based around the use of computerised infrared measuring heads that are fitted to each wheel. The wheels are then checked for run-out (buckling). The next series of checks produces a computerised printout of: toe, castor, king pin inclination, and wheel setback for the front wheels, and toe, thrust angle and camber for the rear wheels. A copy of the information is yours to keep for reference, and as a starting point for any rectification you need to undertake.

ORDER OF DECISIONS FOR MAKING CHANGES TO THE SUSPENSION

Having covered the basics of car suspension it's time to move on to planning some solutions:

1. Identify major problems (alignment and suspension checks).
2. Make wheel and tyre selection.
3. Ride height.
4. Spring stiffness (front and rear).
5. Roll stiffness (front and rear).
6. Damping.
7. Compliance (bush) stiffness.
8. Camber changes.
9. Steering system changes.

RIDE HEIGHT

Reductions in ride height will reduce body roll because the centre of gravity is lowered. There is also a benefit in that pitch will also be reduced. Lastly, there may also be a reduction in the amount of air travelling under the car, thereby improving the coefficient of drag and increasing straight line top speed. Ride height is generally controlled by the springs (whatever form they take: torsion bars, hydragas units, etc), though the wheel and tyre combination can also change it. If the

car has coil springs, a change in their height (or the heights of their mounting platforms) will change the ride height of the car. Whatever the spring rate on your car, it will be possible to purchase an after market spring set identical in every respect other than overall height. However, since most lowered springs are also uprated as well, you may well need to establish spring rates in conjunction with ride height. If you are happy with a spring rate, but cannot get springs in the height you want, and are not keen on the expense of having a set of bespoke springs made, you can consider lowering their installed height by using some kind of spacer to lower the spring pan (where possible). If you are really desperate, you can cut a set of coil springs to shorten them but it's not recommended. **Warning!** - Note that if you have load-controlled ABS on the rear wheels, you may need to have the setting of the system checked and adjusted by a specialist garage or main dealer.

Generally speaking, it is best to

choose replacement springs with a rate that closely matches the original fitments, as the car's manufacturers went to great trouble to find the best spring rates for the car. If you choose stiffer springs, be aware that they'll have a detrimental effect on the car's ride qualities.

Other types of spring can be set lower, as is the case with torsion bars and hydragas units, by resetting them in accordance with the workshop manual or the work can be done by a main dealer.

The bare minimum alignment check should be the front wheel tracking which has just been done here.

Standard and lowered cars nose-to-nose for comparison. (Courtesy - Flyin' Miata)

SPRING RATES

The spring rate - the strength of the spring (usually expressed in pounds), particularly at the front of the car - should be considered as part of the overall modifications to the car, not just suspension modifications. This is because changes to the overall weight of the car change the degree to which the springs have to work. For instance, if you are swapping engines - such as cast iron four cylinder to alloy V8 - the all-up weight of the car may actually be lighter because the alloy V8, although a larger engine, is lighter than the original. On the other hand, if you are fitting a heavy in car entertainment (ICE) system, the overall weight of the car will increase. That said, the amount of increased spring stiffness you can live with will depend largely on your own preference.

In addition to the all-up weight of the car, the springs need to be considered in relation to the anti-roll bars (where fitted). It is always better to reduce roll by increasing anti-roll bar size (diameter) rather than spring stiffness.

Before buying springs, take a look in the workshop manual for your car and find out what the standard spring rate is for your model. Then consider whether the existing springs are so old that they might be soft, and all the car really needs is new springs of the original rate, rather than something harder. This is likely to be the case, especially if you have increased the roll stiffness with stiffer anti-roll bars. It's possible to have a spring checked to find out what its rate is. However, you may well find that none of your local garages have this piece of equipment and, if this is the case, try a local racing team or specialist supplier.

With or without details of your old spring, you can still ask the supplier from whom you plan to purchase your spring, what rates of springs they can offer you.

ANTI-ROLL BARS

One of the most obvious ways to reduce vehicle roll is to increase roll stiffness. One of the best ways to do this is by fitting an anti-roll bar; anti-roll bars are commonly found in the front suspension of the car but sometimes are found on the rear suspension too. The anti-roll bar works by transferring weight from the inside wheel to the outside wheel and thereby resists roll. The reduction in roll reduces changes in tyre camber that are detrimental to the size of the tyre contact patch. The key advantage of the roll bar is not

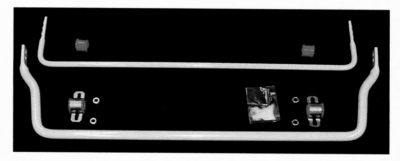

A couple of examples of anti-roll bars both shown with the high performance option of polyurethane bushing, which has much less compliance than rubber. (Courtesy - Flyin' Miata)

SOLVING OR MINIMISING HANDLING PROBLEMS

Problem	Solution
Excessive roll	Fit or uprate anti roll bar Reduce ride height
Excessive pitch	Increase spring rates (stiffness) Reduce ride height
Excessive spring oscillation	Fit new or uprated dampers
General vagueness	Increase compliance (renew or uprate bushes and suspension joints)
Understeer	Increase negative camber Increase toe-out at front (see chapter 14)
Oversteer	Increase toe-in at front (see Chapter 14) Stiffen front anti-roll bar

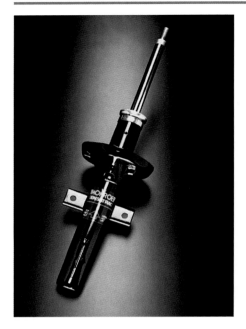

Some dampers, as shown here, form part of a suspension strut. (Courtesy - Tenneco Automotive)

Double wishbones with coil over shock absorber seen here on a Caterham 7.

It is often easier to ensure that the spring and damper match by buying the components in a kit like this one from Whiteline Automotive. (Courtesy - Whiteline Automotive)

just that it reduces roll, but that it only has a pronounced effect when the car does roll. This is unlike the affect of fitting stiffer springs which reduce roll but have a pronounced reaction to road bumps, even when travelling in a straight line.

Once fitted, an anti-roll bar links both sides of the suspension on a single axle. Often, but not always, the anti-roll bar is additionally mounted at a central point on a subframe or chassis section. For vehicles that already have anti-roll bars fitted, it's often possible to further limit roll by increasing the thickness (diameter) of the bar. In addition to the use of a thicker bar, in some instances it's possible to have the rubber in the locating links (where used) replaced with a less compliant material like polyurethane.

Ride height and spring stiffness must be set before selecting an anti-roll bar. The reason for this is that the lower the front end of the car, and the stiffer the front suspension, the less weight transfer there will be, and therefore the less work for the anti-roll bar to do.

Anti-roll bars are rated by thickness, which may be expressed in fractions of an imperial inch or in millimetres. Note, though, that just a few millimetres or sixteenths of an inch can double the stiffness of the bar so, when testing for the optimum bar size, only go up a size at a time. The reason for this is that stiffness increases as a fourth power of change in diameter. Put another way, you have to multiply the diameter four times to calculate a stiffness value. For imperial bars you will need to convert the diameter to the metric equivalent. As an example, a 22mm bar gives an end value of 234,256, while a 26mm bar has a value of 456,976 (i.e. 26 x 26 x 26 x 26). You can see then, that while the

26mm bar is only slightly thicker it is almost twice as stiff.

Should you find your requirement is for something in between the diameters commercially available, locate a specialist supplier that will make a one-off bar for you.

BUSHES & JOINTS

When the bushes or suspension joints are old and worn, the suspension will have more compliance that it was designed to have, and handling will suffer. Replacement of worn out parts will produce an instant benefit. For improvements beyond fitting new parts, it's possible to get uprated bushes which have less compliance than standard for certain makes and models. A stiffer medium for bushes than rubber is polyurethane and several suppliers exist that have a wide range of replacements and can accommodate most makes and models. Nylatron and similar hard plastic materials are also widely available for many applications. The use of Nylatron as a bushing material, however, is not recommended for road use as it is much too stiff. Likewise, spherical rod end bearings (Rose joints) are also not recommended for road use because they are insufficiently compliant.

Be aware that if you use stiffer bushes the car's NVH (noise, vibration, and harshness) levels will increase.

SHOCK ABSORBERS (DAMPERS) - GENERAL

At each 'corner' of the car there will be a shock absorber to go with each spring. The shock absorber's job is to damp the oscillations of the spring to ensure that the wheel and tyre stay in contact with the road. If uprated springs are fitted to a car, then an increase in damping stiffness is also required to go with them. However,

even on their own, changes to the shock absorbers can produce useful benefits in ride, handling, and braking. In fact, you can often improve the overall performance of your car simply by replacing standard units that are worn. If just one shock absorber is faulty (perhaps only working at 50 per cent efficiency) the ride, handling and braking will suffer to a marked degree. With just one defective shock absorber a car will typically require an extra 8.5 feet to brake to a standstill from 50mph. With worn shocks, aquaplaning (loss of grip in wet), can start at speeds 10mph lower than for a car with good shocks. However, perhaps of greatest interest, when cornering on a tight bend (at 50mph) the rear end of the car can break traction at 5mph less than a car with good shocks. Finally, consider that once a car has covered 40,000 miles the shock absorbers should be checked for wear every 12,000 miles.

Warning! - If a shock absorber does need replacement, always also replace the other shock absorber on the same axle. When you come to choose a replacement unit consider the difference between ordinary and gas units. Contrary to popular belief, both ordinary and gas units will have oil in them. It is the action of the shock absorber piston (with its associated valving) travelling through the oil, that damps the action of the spring. With a conventional unit the interaction between the oil and air causes the oil to foam, thereby reducing damping action and leading to the phenomenon of shock absorber fade (a markedly reduced efficiency). With a gas unit there is no foaming and hence no fade. However, note that under very extreme conditions, such as special stage rallying, fade can still occur with a standard gas unit.

Coil over shocks from Edelbrock. (Courtesy - Edelbrock)

This Eibach Pro Kit includes all the major suspension components to lower and stiffen the suspension. (Courtesy - Eibach)

Some dampers, like this AVO, are on-car adjustable.

Shock absorbers (dampers) - uprated

When fitting uprated shocks you normally increase ride control at the expense of ride comfort. The only exception to this rule is the Monroe Sensatrac. The Sensatrac is unique in that the action of the piston in the shock absorber tube is not just controlled by the valves in the piston. It has a vertical groove in the wall of the shock absorber which allows the oil to flow between the top and bottom of the shock absorber tube, thereby bypassing the piston - this allows for a faster, and therefore softer, damping action. However, in order to retain a slower, and therefore firmer, damping action, the groove only exists at the 'comfort zone' of damper travel where the wheel movements are small. When wheel movements are large, the piston moves into the 'control zone' where no groove exists and normal piston action occurs, and with the Sensatrac this means a firm damping action. In use, the Sensatrac truly offers the best of both worlds - race stiffness with road softness.

The Monroe Sensatrac is ideally suited to a fast road car by virtue of its special design with comfort zone shown here ... (Courtesy - Tenneco Automotive)

... and here. (Courtesy - Tenneco Automotive)

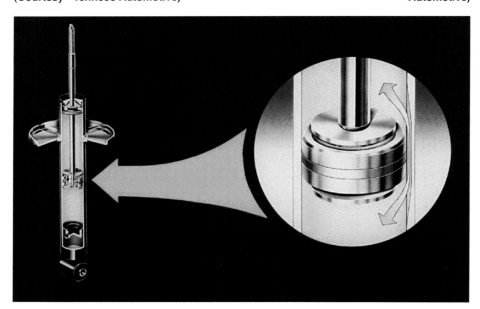

Chapter 14

Front suspension & steering

INTRODUCTION

It's obvious that performance modifications to the front suspension (in isolation) and steering will improve the cornering of the vehicle. But, other than for a few exceptions covered in this chapter, guidance in the preceding chapter will stand good for front and rear suspension.

CAMBER CHANGES

If your car has MacPherson strut front suspension it is possible to change the camber by means of an adjustable top mount. In the UK Flow Tech Racing and HKS are the only companies I know of who manufacture special top mounting brackets that will allow camber changes. Once you have decided which make of shock absorbers you are going to use, you can purchase to suit. The new top mounting will replace the old, but setting-up will require access to a camber gauge or will need to be carried out in conjunction with a follow-up alignment check.

Most cars that don't have MacPherson strut suspension will have some method of camber adjustment built into them.

TRACKING

Sometimes known as 'toe' (as in pigeon toed) because tracking refers to how much out of parallel with each other the wheels on an axle are. Although rear wheel toe is often not

Available from HKS for most Japanese cars it is possible to use a similar adjustable top mount. (Courtesy - HKS)

adjustable, front toe always is. If the fronts of the wheels are closer together than the rears, they are said to 'toe-in'. Generally, as little toe-in as possible is preferred (even toe-out - the reverse of toe-in - may produce the best handling results). However, each car will be different, and you should be guided by standard settings for any suspension modification you undertake. The tracking can be set as part of a total alignment check, or by a garage with tracking equipment.

STRUT BRACES

Strut braces are often seen as a fashion accessory for show under the bonnet. Though it may be the case that they look smart, they do, in fact, serve an important function; what the strut brace does is link the top front suspension mountings together, usually on a car with MacPherson struts. What this linking does is reduce chassis flex and thereby reduces spurious wheel alignment changes mid-corner.

This is typical of suspension with a wishbone acting as the suspension bottom link, with a MacPherson strut damper and spring unit acting as the top link, which would fit into the vehicle inner wing.

A strut brace like the very neat Jamex item shown here increases the rigidity of the car and minimises unwanted suspension geometry changes. (Courtesy - Jamex)

For MacPherson strut front suspension it is possible to fit this adjustable mount from Australian specialist Whiteline Automotive to adjust vehicle camber. (Courtesy - Whiteline Automotive)

STEERING - GENERAL

To a large extent, how well the car responds to the steering input will depend on the car's suspension and tyres. This section, therefore, is about the steering input part of the equation. In practice this means the steering wheel, steering column, and steering rack.

Steering wheel

The steering wheel is one of the primary car control devices, and one often taken for granted. Size matters with the steering wheel, the smaller the diameter of the wheel the quicker the driver can input steering commands - and the heavier the steering. Do not confuse inputting steering commands with the vehicle's response to them. Just because the driver can input a steering command quickly does not mean the vehicle will respond quickly

because steering response is a function of the wheels, tyres, and suspension components. However, if the vehicle can respond quicker than you can input steering commands to it, for example because the steering wheel has an enormous diameter, then there may be some merit in choosing a smaller diameter replacement.

Note that what is a good size steering wheel for one vehicle might not be the case for another. One example of this would be swapping a steering wheel from a RWD vehicle to a FWD vehicle. The reason for this is that FWD vehicles usually have a quicker steering response than RWD vehicles. A quite different reason is that steering rack ratios also vary from car to car (more of this later).

Dimensionally, steering wheels vary from 10 to 16 inches (usually going up an inch at a time) or from 260mm to 350mm. In both cases the smallest sizes are really only suited to racing cars. Typically, a good choice of size would be between 12 to 14 inches, or the nearest metric equivalent.

Another consideration regarding your steering wheel is not its dimension but its dishing. Dish is the difference in depth between the steering wheel centre and the rim. The choice is usually between flat or dished, though sometimes a deep dish is available. On the face of it you might think it is simpler to move the seat nearer the wheel to adjust for arm reach. However, some models, makes, and individuals, have an arrangement which is less than comfortable for quick driving. If such circumstances apply to you, set the seat position to the pedals, and then choose a steering wheel to give the reach you require. Of course, if your car has an adjustable steering column, then dish really shouldn't matter.

Finally, a problem with more

modern cars are models equipped with air bags. **Warning!** - If your car has an air bag, then it is best to leave the steering wheel alone, until such time as after market manufacturers introduce air bag steering wheels.

Steering column
The steering column carries the steering inputs to the steering rack or box and usually requires no modification whatsoever. However, it is possible to have a steering column shortened, though the associated modifications require considerable thought before proceeding with the job.

STEERING RATIOS
The steering ratio is found by seeing how many turns and part turns of the steering wheel there are from lock to lock. To establish what the standard ratio is on your car, turn the steering to full lock in one direction and then count the turns until it is on the full opposite lock. Note that a smaller diameter steering wheel does not change the ratio of the rack, but does change the amount your hands move to achieve it. A fast ratio is one that has

2.5 turns lock to lock. Although some road cars do have slightly faster ratios than this, the majority will have more. Rally Design is one company I know of that supplies exchange 'fast' racks and conversion kits to convert a rack to a 2.5 ratio.

POWER-ASSISTED STEERING RACKS
If you have fitted a small diameter steering wheel and a fast rack to your car, you might have a steering action which is nice and fast, and is just what you want. Alternatively, you might have left the steering standard but fitted wider wheels and tyres. It is possible, however, that a combination of any of these factors may have introduced the unpleasant side effect of

heavy steering. (It's worth checking the steering with the front of the car jacked up, just to ensure that the heavy steering isn't caused by unlubricated or worn out parts.) Another cause of heavy steering is underinflated tyres. If everything is in order mechanically, and the tyre pressures are OK, there are two solutions. The first is to spend some time working out with weights to strengthen your arms. The second is to find out whether you can fit a power-assisted steering rack. If another model or variant of your car has PAS it's worth investigating whether it can be fitted to your car. Your local dealer/parts outlet should be able to advise if this is possible.

It is possible to replace the standard steering rack with a quick rack like the one shown here available from Rally Design. (Courtesy - Rally Design)

Chapter 15

Rear suspension

INTRODUCTION

The main aspect of performance affected by the rear suspension is, predictably, cornering speed. However, because of weight changes, which might easily be gains as well as losses, acceleration and deceleration are also affected. Depending on the drive configuration of your car there will either be a little or a lot that can be done by way of improvement.

If the car is FWD the rear suspension will consist of springs (which may be torsion bars) and dampers acting on some form of axle with little scope for improvement. With a RWD car, particularly older models, there may be a live axle arrangement which will have scope for large improvements. Other RWD cars and 4WD cars will have a final drive unit and driveshafts incorporated as part of the overall rear suspension design which may offer some scope for improvement, but less than a live axle arrangement.

LIVE AXLE WITH LEAF SPRINGS

Of all the rear suspension designs, the live axle and leaf spring arrangement has the greatest potential for improvement. It is also a design found on a whole range of cars that are likely to be developed for fast road use.

The reason that you can do so much to improve this set-up is that it suffers from a couple of inbuilt detriments to good handling, and it is also heavy. The top four options table below can be used as a guide, and option three can also be used in conjunction with other RWD suspension systems

TOP FOUR OPTIONS FOR IMPROVING LIVE AXLE SUSPENSION (WITH LEAF SPRINGS)

1. Renew all existing bushes with new items, preferably in polyurethane.
2. Fit anti-tramp bars.
3. Fit a Panhard rod or Watts linkage.

4. Convert suspension to four link design (doing away with the leaf springs).

Anti-tramp bars

If you have a sufficiently powerful engine in a car with a leaf sprung live axle, and use it in anger for standing starts or traffic light grands prix, you will most likely experience what is known as axle tramp/hop, or at least your car will. What happens is that the torque being transmitted to the rear wheels from the axle causes the axle to twist the springs into a shallow S-shape. The springs then release the stored energy, twisting the axle in the reverse direction. This process is repeated until the torque loading is released from the springs. As you accelerate it feels like the back axle is jumping up and down (which is exactly what it's doing). Besides being detrimental to good acceleration, axle tramp can break the differential carrier of some axles and needs to be prevented. I have heard that tramp

because they increase the overall weight of the vehicle. Therefore, if you can afford it, a far better and neater solution is to convert the rear axle to a four link system with coil springs, but more of that later.

PANHARD RODS & WATTS LINKAGES

The leaf springs, when used in conjunction with a live axle, do more than just provide springing, they also locate the axle as well, usually by U-bolts and nuts at the spring's mid-length point. Each end of the spring is fixed to the car to locate the whole assembly. Although this mounting arrangement holds the axle in place, the compliance is such that the axle has some side-to-side movement which is undesirable. This will most likely be felt as a looseness or fishtailing action

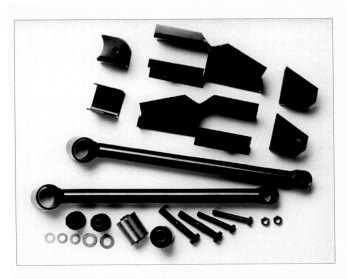

Typical anti-tramp bar kit. (Courtesy - Rally Design)

MacPherson struts on rear suspension are sometimes known as 'Chapman struts' and are shown here on this car which has been sectioned for display purposes.

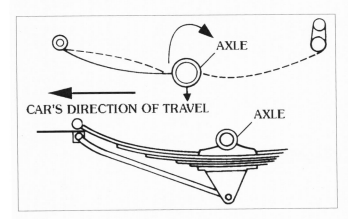

With a live axle and leaf springs rotational forces on the axle can twist or wind up the spring, resulting in axle tramp or hop. (Drawn by Dave Robinson/Sharon Monroe)

can be reduced on some cars by fitting nylatron bushes in the spring eyes but, generally, the most effective solution (without doing away with the leaf springs) is to fit anti-tramp bars.

Anti-tramp bars are a pair of bars, one for the forward half of each leaf spring, that connect at one end to the car bodywork and to the centre of the spring at the other. The anti-tramp bar brackets can be mounted in conjunction with the leaf spring mountings and are connected by a rigid bar or tube to form the complete

assembly. Anti-tramp bars work by preventing distortion of the leaf spring. If the bars can be designed such that the mounting brackets are not just mounted in conjunction with other brackets but as part of them (a hybrid bracket), then the end product will be lighter. Some cars have purpose-built after market kits available for them. In other instances you'll need to approach a local fabricator to have them make the bars for you.

Fitting anti-tramp bars is not the best solution to solving axle tramp

when driving through fast S-bends or any bend series. Note that it can be the case that the worn rubbers in the spring eyes are creating these same symptoms and replacement rubbers or, perhaps, polyurethane bushes will cure the fault - check this first.

Dead axle FWD and non-live axle RWD cars may also suffer from inadequate sideways location but, generally speaking, inadequate sideways location can be addressed by fitting a Panhard rod or a Watts linkage. A Panhard rod is a rod which has one

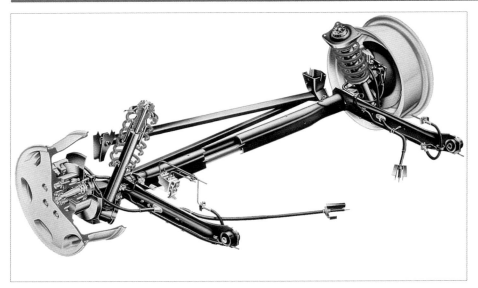

A live axle (RWD) with a Watts linkage for lateral stability; note also the twin coil over dampers for this heavy American car.

In this illustration of the Audi 100 rear axle assembly, which is a 'dead' axle, you can see the Panhard rod. (Courtesy - V.A.G. (UK) Ltd)

Brackets for a Panhard rod, this one is for the RWD Escort from Rally Design. (Courtesy - Rally Design)

end connected to the car's chassis and the other to one end of the axle. By forming a rigid connection between the car and the axle sideways movement is prevented. A Watts linkage performs the same job as the Panhard rod but has a rod fixed to each end of the axle with a central body-mounted pivot point above the centre of the axle. For non-live axle RWD and FWD with dead axle cars the arrangements are similar, but with one end of the pickup on a hard suspension mounting point rather than the live axle. For cars well known to benefit from the fitting of either item, an after market kit will be available. In other cases it will be a case of having something specially fabricated.

FOUR LINK SUSPENSION CONVERSIONS

Because of the drawbacks of leaf springs and a live axle, a conversion to four links and coil springs has considerable merit. This design works by using upper and lower axle locating links each side of the axle, thereby replacing the locating function of the leaf springs. Coil springs are then located on the axle at each side to provide springing, thereby replacing the second function of the leaf spring. Coil springs can also be used in conjunction with shock absorbers to form a single unit ('coil over' shocks). The disadvantage to converting to this configuration is that, in most cases, you'll need to find a good workshop that can design and fabricate a system for you or do it yourself, unless you have a RWD Ford Escort for which conversion kits are available. For a variety of American cars there are purpose built conversion kits available from Art Morrison Ltd.

It is possible, though, to offer some general guidance on four link conversions. The first job will be to work out where the spring coils and shock absorbers need to be located. They will need to be as near the axle ends as possible, but without fouling any other component such as the tyre. They will generally need to merge into the wheel well at some point, perhaps to the full extent of their height and, at the top, will intrude into the car. The orientation of the coil and shock ideally needs to be vertical. However, if that causes problems, they can lean slightly from the vertical either side to side or front to back. It will soon be apparent that where the top of the coil shocks need to be located inside the car, if not fouling something, is thin air. To provide a mounting for

A 4 link kit for the RWD Escort, again from Rally Design. (Courtesy - Rally Design)

the shock a turret box will need to be fabricated. Once all of this work has been completed you can experiment with springs, damper settings, and ride heights. Although ride is a matter of personal preference it's recommended to start with a setting 10 per cent harder than the manufacturer's standard.

RIDE HEIGHT
You'll need to read the 'Ride Height' section of the 'Suspension - General' chapter before embarking on any modifications to ride height, and decide by how much you want to lower it. You also need to know what sort of rear suspension your car has.

Leaf sprung rear ends are probably the easiest to lower, and the usual method is to insert a lowering block between the axle and the spring. The drawback to this method is that it can either introduce or exacerbate axle tramp. An alternative is, of course, to change the springs altogether for

some flatter ones. If flatter arches are not commercially available, the existing springs can be re-tempered and re-cambered to produce a reduced ride height. A neater method of reducing ride height with leaf springs is to reduce the height of the front spring shackle. This can be difficult to achieve and may require expert fabrication of new, modified, front hanger brackets. Don't be tempted to try the same trick on the rear brackets because, although the lowering effect is the same, it changes the suspension geometry unfavourably.

Coil sprung rear ends are even easier to lower than leaf spring rear ends, all that is required is the purchase of shorter springs. It is possible to cut springs but, quite frankly, is the aggravation really worth it? On some installations it's possible to lower the spring at the bottom mounting by using spacers between the pan and the wishbone. Another possibility is that some after market shock absorbers (coil-over-type) have adjustable spring seats.

Torsion bar rear suspension is fiddly to lower but generally will involve no new parts and, therefore, expense. Clean up the end of the torsion bar where you are going to make the adjustment, and paint or

mark a line for the standard position. Next, follow the workshop procedure for removing the suspension arm from the torsion bar, and, when you refit the arm, put the spline one tooth around from the original setting. Repeat this procedure until you get the desired ride height.

DAMPING - ALL TYPES OF SUSPENSION
The 'Suspension - General' chapter has guidance on damping (shock absorbers).

ANTI-ROLL BARS - ALL TYPES OF SUSPENSION
On some cars, usually FWD ones, a rear anti-roll bar is fitted to reduce understeer by creating a degree of compensating oversteer. Any existing anti-roll bar can be stiffened by using solid (aluminium) or stiffer (nylatron or polyurethane) mountings, or it can be replaced by a thicker bar. However, it is probably a better idea to spend time and money minimising the front end understeer before considering fitting an anti-roll bar to the rear of a car without one, or increasing the size of the bar on a car that does.

REAR WHEEL ALIGNMENT
With a live axle car there is no scope for adjustment of rear wheel alignment. On some cars with independent rear suspension it is possible to make some adjustments to both camber and tracking at the rear though this may not be a DIY proposition - the general suspension section offers advice on this point.

Chapter 16
Wheels & tyres

INTRODUCTION

For any fast road car, the wheel and tyre combination is crucial to all aspects of the car's performance. Biggest is generally best, and the more rubber you can put on the road the better. The limitations on how much rubber you can put down will vary from car to car, and to an extent, the weight of the car and the power output of the engine will dictate a reasonable size range. However, it is easy to make a poor choice or find that having made your purchase, it is not what you want after all. To avoid such errors, the accompanying table suggests a logical order in which to make your decisions. The remainder of this chapter will provide all the information you need to help you select wheels and tyres, as well as supplementary information on related issues.

ORDER OF DECISIONS FOR MAKING WHEEL & TYRE SELECTION

1. Overall diameter of the tyre (note lower profile means smaller diameter).
2. Tyre profile.
3. Tyre width.
4. Actual tyre including speed rating.
5. Wheel diameter to tie in with choices 1 and 2 (note if 2 becomes a higher value so does 1).
6. Stud pattern (Pitch Circle Diameter).
7. Wheel rim width, inset and offset (bearing in mind 3).
8. Style of wheel.

TYRES

Given that the tyres should be chosen before the wheels it makes sense to look at the tyres first. Tyres are diverse in size and type and each tyre comes complete with a bundle of useful but coded information on the sidewall. The 'writing on the wall' illustration shows all the markings which may appear on a tyre sidewall, and covers both European and North American standards. The markings likely to be of most interest are those which indicate size, speed and load rating. A typical size designation might be 185/70HR14. The first number in our example is 185 and this indicates the nominal width of the tyre in millimetres. The number 70 indicates the aspect ratio which is the percentage of nominal section height to nominal section width. The letter 'H' indicates the speed rating. The letter 'R' indicates the tyre is of radial ply construction (it will be rare to find a crossply construction tyre today). Finally, the last two numbers indicate the wheel rim diameter the tyre is intended for.

TYRE SPEED RATING

Warning! - Each and every type of tyre has a maximum safe running speed so, if performance modifications have increased the top speed capability of your car, you must check that the tyres are appropriately rated to

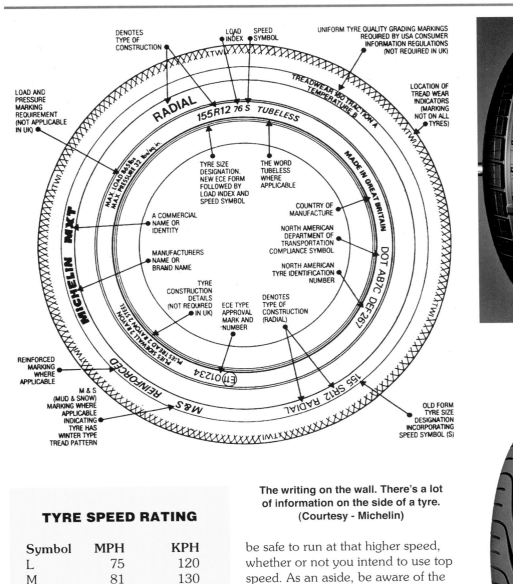

The writing on the wall. There's a lot of information on the side of a tyre.
(Courtesy - Michelin)

Diagram labels:

- DENOTES TYPE OF CONSTRUCTION
- LOAD INDEX
- SPEED SYMBOL
- UNIFORM TYRE QUALITY GRADING MARKINGS REQUIRED BY USA CONSUMER INFORMATION REGULATIONS (NOT REQUIRED IN UK)
- LOAD AND PRESSURE MARKING REQUIREMENT (NOT APPLICABLE IN UK)
- RADIAL
- 155R12 76 S TUBELESS
- TREADWEAR 160 TRACTION A TEMPERATURE B
- LOCATION OF TREAD WEAR INDICATORS (MARKING NOT ON ALL TYRES)
- MAX. LOAD 615 lbs MAX PRESSURE 32 lbs/sq. in.
- TYRE SIZE DESIGNATION. NEW ECE FORM FOLLOWED BY LOAD INDEX AND SPEED SYMBOL
- THE WORD TUBELESS WHERE APPLICABLE
- MADE IN GREAT BRITAIN
- A COMMERCIAL NAME OR IDENTITY
- COUNTRY OF MANUFACTURE
- MANUFACTURERS NAME OR BRAND NAME
- NORTH AMERICAN DEPARTMENT OF TRANSPORTATION COMPLIANCE SYMBOL
- NORTH AMERICAN TYRE IDENTIFICATION NUMBER
- TYRE CONSTRUCTION DETAILS (NOT REQUIRED IN UK)
- ECE TYPE APPROVAL MARK AND NUMBER
- DENOTES TYPE OF CONSTRUCTION (RADIAL)
- DOT AB7C DEF 267
- MICHELIN MXT
- PLIES SIDEWALL 2 RAYON PLIES TREAD 2 RAYON 2 STEEL
- (E11) 01234
- M&S REINFORCED
- 155 SR12 RADIAL
- REINFORCED MARKING WHERE APPLICABLE
- M & S (MUD & SNOW) MARKING WHERE APPLICABLE INDICATING TYRE HAS WINTER TYPE TREAD PATTERN
- OLD FORM TYRE SIZE DESIGNATION INCORPORATING SPEED SYMBOL (S)

The A008P from Yokohama.

TYRE SPEED RATING

Symbol	MPH	KPH
L	75	120
M	81	130
N	87	140
P	93	150
Q	100	160
R	106	170
S	112	180
T	118	190
U	124	200
H	130	210
V	149	240
W	167	270
Y	186	300

be safe to run at that higher speed, whether or not you intend to use top speed. As an aside, be aware of the maximum permitted running speeds of space saver-type spare wheels. The accompanying table provides all the information you need.

OVERALL SIZE

When considering what size wheel and tyre combination to fit, there are a number of constraints, and therefore a number of decisions, which need to be made and planned for. The overriding constraint on overall diameter of

**Another choice of performance tyre is the Goodyear Eagle F1.
(Courtesy - Goodyear Dunlop)**

Something a bit different - chrome wire spoked wheels shown here on a Mazda MX-5 with Pirelli P7 tyre. (Courtesy - MWS Ltd)

the wheel and tyre combination is whether or not you want to undertake bodywork modifications to allow a larger wheel and tyre to fit. If you are prepared to undertake bodywork modifications then, within reason, most widths can be accommodated, using spacers if necessary, more of which later. The restriction on overall diameter is dictated partly by what is available, the size of the car, and how little suspension travel you can live with. The important thing to consider is practicality and cost.

TYRE OVERALL DIAMETER, PROFILE & WIDTH

The overriding constraint on overall diameter of the tyres is whether or not you want to undertake bodywork, braking, suspension, and, maybe, gearing modifications to allow the use of a larger overall diameter. Once you have decided on the overall tyre diameter, you must consider a tyre profile size. In other words, you have already decided on diameter, now you must decide how much rubber you want between the tread surface of the tyre and the wheel rim. Note that the marked tyre size is based on the wheel diameter and not the diameter of the tyre itself. The greater the amount of rubber between the tyre tread surface and the rim (higher profile, higher number) the more comfortable the ride will be, but with correspondingly less driving response. The less rubber (lower profile, lower number) the sharper the response, but the harsher the ride. Depending on your choice of overall diameter and profile you may or may not be able to change to a different profile in the future without running into clearance

The Dunlop Super Sport. (Courtesy - Goodyear Dunlop)

The Dunlop SP Sport Max. (Courtesy - Goodyear Dunlop)

problems that can only be negated by changing wheel diameter. For instance, if you have tyres of 60 profile you can change to tyres of 50 profile with a resultant smaller rolling radius on the same wheel. However, if you have tyres of 40 profile a change to tyres of 50 profile will increase the overall rolling radius unless you switch to a smaller diameter wheel. Whatever your final choice, once it is made, bear in mind that it will be expensive, or possibly very expensive, to change to something different.

As far as tyre width goes, widest is best, except for loose surface and snow conditions. For road use, be realistic about the performance capability of the car, your own driving ability, and the motoring laws of your country, and not least how much the extra width will

cost. **Warning!** - Another important consideration is that an increase in tyre width is likely to create clearance problems and under no circumstances must the tyre contact any part of the car, be it bodywork, brake components or suspension components: it may

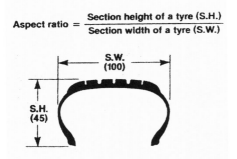

$$\text{Aspect ratio} = \frac{\text{Section height of a tyre (S.H.)}}{\text{Section width of a tyre (S.W.)}}$$

Aspect ratio measures section height to section width. (Courtesy - Yokohma)

also be illegal for the tyre to protrude beyond the bodywork. But if you are prepared to undertake or pay for bodywork modifications such as wheelarch flares, then most sensible tyre widths can be accommodated. In addition, clearance problems can be overcome by careful choice of wheel inset/offset or wheel spacers.

TYRE PRESSURES

As important as your tyre selection is the air pressure you put in the tyres. Note that tyre pressures should always be checked cold. Generally speaking, an increase in tyre pressure will improve the handling of the car. Try inflating tyres to 10 per cent over the recommended pressures for fast driving. However, in some instances, better performance may be achieved

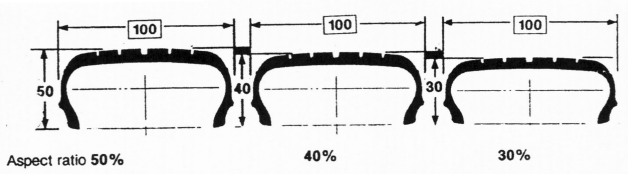

Aspect ratio 50%   **40%**   **30%**

As illustrated, holding section width constant, section height will decrease as aspect ratio decreases. (Courtesy - Yokohma)

Holding rim diameter constant, overall diameter (and ride height) will decrease as apect ratio decreases. (Courtesy - Yokohama)

by reducing pressure but never by more than two or three pounds below the manufacturers' recommended setting. **Caution!** - Whichever pressure setting you use, be extremely careful not to overdo it as the tyre may be damaged permanently. Over inflation causes excessive tension in the casing cords which makes the tyre more vulnerable to impact damage. Over inflation by 20 per cent has been found to cause a 10 per cent reduction in tyre life (by wear). Under inflation allows excessive flexing and rapid overheating, leading eventually to casing break-up and failure. Under inflation by 10 per cent has been found to cause a 26 per cent reduction in tyre life (by wear). There is unfortunately no golden rule for starting pressure for tyres, but generally a cold pressure of 20psi is a minimum, while 32psi is a maximum (**Warning!** - always consult the tyre manufacturer for advice on optimal pressures). For guidance as to the effect of variation of tyre pressures on handling consult the accompanying table regarding tyre pressures.

WHEEL WIDTH, DIAMETER & WEIGHT

Having made your choice of tyre, you now need to find a wheel that will suit it. There are a number of constraints and decisions which need to be made and planned for. Also, for any given tyre width there is a minimum and maximum rim size that will accommodate it. Wheel weight is very important - not just the part it plays in overall vehicle weight, or even unsprung weight, but because the wheel is accelerated twice, initially as it revolves, and then, as it moves forward as part of the car. Obviously, the larger the wheel the more it will weigh. Wheels are generally made from steel, aluminium alloy or magnesium alloy. 'Alloy wheels' is the general but

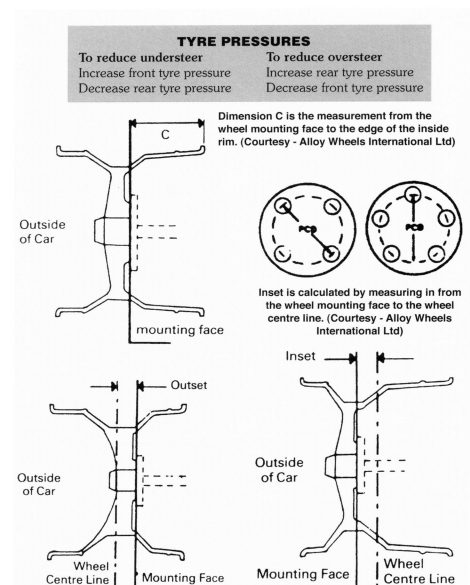

TYRE PRESSURES

To reduce understeer	To reduce oversteer
Increase front tyre pressure	Increase rear tyre pressure
Decrease rear tyre pressure	Decrease front tyre pressure

Dimension C is the measurement from the wheel mounting face to the edge of the inside rim. (Courtesy - Alloy Wheels International Ltd)

Inset is calculated by measuring in from the wheel mounting face to the wheel centre line. (Courtesy - Alloy Wheels International Ltd)

The Pitch Circle Diameter (PCD) is the diameter of the circle that passes through the centre of all the wheel studs or bolt holes. (Courtesy - Alloy Wheels International Ltd)

Outset is calculated by measuring out from the wheel mounting face to the wheel centre line. (Courtesy - Alloy Wheels International Ltd)

imprecise term for aluminium alloy wheels and there is a huge selection to choose from. Magnesium alloy wheels are the lightest, but are expensive. One interesting choice are bolt-on

wire spoked wheels. By no means the performance option because of their weight, they are nonetheless one choice of wheel that stands out from the crowd, especially if chromed. Unlike the original knock-off wire wheels that cannot usually be used with low profile tyres, the modern equivalents can, but check before purchasing.

The most important consideration regarding your new wheels is that they should have appropriate inset or offset to give the same wheel centreline as the original equipment wheels. Going outboard of the original centreline is acceptable to a degree, but will increase wheel bearing loads and for FWD cars can cause steering problems under power. **Warning!** - The new wheels must not contact any brake/suspension components or the bodywork.

WHEEL STUD OR BOLT PATTERN

Whatever wheels you choose, the stud or bolt pattern will have to be the same as the existing wheels unless you are going to change the hubs (where possible) for ones with a different stud or bolt pattern. The name for stud or bolt pattern is 'Pitch Circle Diameter' (PCD).

WHEEL SPACERS, STUDS, BOLTS & NUTS

Wheel spacers are often frowned upon as being a cause of premature wheel bearing failure, and certainly the use of a spacer will not extend bearing life. However, given that the use of spacers may allow higher cornering forces, all things being equal, then higher loads are going to be placed on the wheel bearings anyway.

The actual thickness of the spacer can vary enormously, usually they are between 10mm and 30mm each. When using spacers, a point to watch is that there is no tyre to wheelarch contact. Of course, if you are using a spacer to allow fitment of a wheel that does not have the right backface, then you should have allowed for the total

Low profile tyres on big wheels gives potential for bigger brakes.

clearance necessary anyway.

Warning! - Once you have decided on the spacer thickness, you must get studs (or bolts) of a longer length to match. Note that it is possible to get studs (or bolts) of a greater thickness than standard to ensure that the overall strength of the stud isn't compromised, but you may need to modify other wheel components, or even the wheels

A typical wheel spacer, this one from Jamex, is used to increase the wheel track of the vehicle or create clearance for brake calipers etc. (Courtesy - Jamex)

Just one wheel design of many from TSW. (Courtesy - Yokohama H.P.T. Ltd)

For popular models like the Mazda MX-5/Miata there will always be a wide range of after market alloy wheels to choose from. (Courtesy - Flyin' Miata)

themselves, before using them.

Wheel nuts, other than locking ones fitted for protection against theft, are usually replaced with nonstandard items for aesthetic reasons rather than performance considerations. However, for many types of alloy wheels you'll need to purchase special nuts to go with the wheels themselves.

Finally, if your vehicle has bolts to fix the wheels to the hubs, it is possible to convert to studs and nuts in some cases. Trans Auto Sport manufactures kits which are retailed through most popular motor factors.

Chapter 17
Electrics & instruments

INTRODUCTION

There are no improvements to aspects of performance associated with electrics and instruments. However, there are some electrical considerations associated with tuning, such as ensuring the engine will always start, for example. Instrumentation is important because a tuned engine needs to be monitored more accurately and closely than a standard engine, and under heavy loads its operating temperatures (oil and coolant) can increase significantly quicker than would those of a standard engine. The value of other improvements and modifications detailed in this chapter is self-explanatory.

ELECTRONIC DASHBOARDS

If you have a fully electronic dashboard there is not much you can do to it yourself by way of modification - if you have a problem with it you'll need expert help. A change of gearing, because of a change in gearbox or differential ratios, or even the size of the wheel and tyre combinations, will all cause speedometer inaccuracy. Engine or ignition system changes can cause problems with the tachometer. Because electronic dashboards are programmed, you cannot simply have instruments recalibrated, they need reprogramming. One company that can help you, possibly the only company, is Digi Dash.

SPEEDOMETER MODIFICATIONS

If your car has quite an old design of speedometer and it has been tuned to go much faster than standard you may have problems with speedometer accuracy at higher speeds. It may even be that the new maximum speed of the car is higher than the speedometer calibration.

A change in differential ratio from standard will definitely render the speedometer wildly inaccurate, reading on the slow side for higher gearing and on the fast side for lower gearing - neither is of much use. A change in tyre profiles will have the same effect. In any event, with a tuned road car capable of highly illegal speeds it is preferable to know just how slow or fast your car is travelling. A speedometer can be checked for accuracy on a rolling road and the results noted. However, it's not practical to look at a set of corrected figures whenever you approach the legal speed limit ...

One solution is to use the speedometer from a car similar to yours, perhaps one with a higher top speed, or maybe even a speedometer from a different model of car from the same manufacturer. If this is not possible, because of the design of the speedo and fascia, the only real alternative is to junk the lot and build a purpose-built dash.

If your car has the older type of round speedo unit that fits into a suitable aperture in the dash, life

Everything you might need to give the interior a new look from Jamex. (Courtesy - Jamex)

A nice cluster of gauges including oil temp as well as oil pressure: speeds like this are strictly for track day.

is much easier because a range of circular after market speedometers are commonly available that are as good, if not better, than many cheap original equipment units. In addition, the calibration may be up to an optimistic 160mph! Note, though, that if you have any direction indicator pilot lights, and so on, in the original speedometer unit they will need to be relocated. An alternative to purchasing an after market unit is to visit a breakers yard and find something that will fit your car's aperture, and is capable of recalibration.

Once you have a unit you are happy with it will need recalibration to suit the gearing of the car, and, possibly, a hybrid speedo cable. One company that can carry out this recalibration work is Speedograph Richfield Ltd. To rebuild and recalibrate any unit, with a face to suit, and that is absolutely accurate, they will require you to perform the following steps:

1. Disconnect the speedometer flexible drive at the instrument end.
2. Jack-up one driving wheel and support the car with an axle stand (let them know if your car is fitted with a limited slip diff).
3. Mark suspended driving wheel with a chalk line or masking tape.
4. Mark the rear wing with a similar mark.
5. Make a small arrow from light cardboard and press it onto the end of the speedometer drive inner cable.
6. Revolve the driving wheel by hand exactly twenty times whilst an assistant counts the number of revolutions the inner cable makes to the nearest one eighth of a revolution.
7. Note the make and size of the tyre and the wheel revolution per mile figure if you have it.
8. Send the information from 6 and 7 to Speedograph along with the make (usually Smiths) and part number if legible giving a brief explanation of what your requirement is.

Alternatively they can manufacture and supply a speedometer to suit any particular style or requirement. Another service they provide is that of recalibrating a speedometer from kmh to mph, or vice versa. In addition, as a cable manufacturer, they can produce a speedo cable of any length for your gearbox/speedo combination.

INSTRUMENT GAUGE ILLUMINATION

When you come to wire any supplementary or nonstandard gauge light you will generally find the wire for the bulb's live terminal is red in colour. However, the standard wiring colour for gauge lights on your car is unlikely to be red. In order to have matching wiring, it is necessary to remove the bulb holder from the gauge, remove the bulb and heat the connection with a soldering iron to remove the red (or other colour) wire. The correct colour code wire can be bought from Vehicle Wiring Products Ltd and soldered into the connection as a direct replacement. Once the connection has cooled it can be reinserted into the bulb holder and the bulb holder refitted to the gauge. The easiest way to wire in the supplementary gauge's wire is to fit the bare end of the wire with a bullet connector. Next, cut an existing instrument light wire in two and similarly solder or crimp a bullet connector on each end. The feed and two gauge wires can all be inserted into a two, or if necessary even three, bullet connector block to complete the circuit. A number of alternatives to bullet connectors are available.

OIL PRESSURE WARNING LIGHT

The original oil pressure warning light on your car is usually operated by an oil pressure switch in the engine block which may also operate the oil pressure gauge. Typically, the switch operates at between 3.5lb or 7lb, depending on the switch used, though it may be fractionally greater or lesser than this. As a means of indicating the fact that some oil pressure has been achieved this system is fine, but it is next to useless if a sudden loss of engine oil pressure occurs at high engine speed as, with only 5lb or less of oil pressure, you may have the beginnings of terminal engine damage. To provide earlier warning of low oil pressure, replace the standard switch (where fitted) with a switch that trips at a higher value, 20 or 22lb for example. This higher rated, low pressure oil warning light switch, is available from most high performance component suppliers. For cars with a non-electrical oil pressure gauge system it is possible to replace the standard hose or tube that runs from the union to the gauge with Goodridge braided steel hose made to fit your precise requirement.

An amber dashboard light to indicate low oil pressure, connected in a simple circuit to the pressure switch, should be available from most good component suppliers. It's also possible to wire in a warning buzzer to be activated simultaneously with the light if required.

OIL PRESSURE GAUGE

Although the oil pressure warning light provides indication of low oil pressure, it's desirable to have a constant oil pressure reading available. An oil pressure reading can also be observed in relation to engine temperature, even as a guide to temperature in its own right and, not least, oil pressure when cornering and braking. All of which can provide useful clues to other possible problems, such as oil surge. An oil pressure reading can also be observed and noted over a period of time to give an indication of engine wear.

A gauge is relatively easy to fit by using a suitable union, with an additional outlet for the pressure switch, to replace the standard union fitting. Speedograph Richfield has a range of instrument accessories, one of which should do the job. The piping

for the gauge usually comes with it though, as an alternative, it's possible to employ braided steel hoses, such as Goodridge, with their attendant benefits. Fitting is straightforward, though a point to watch is that the feed pipe to the gauge may need to be bled of excessive air before the gauge will read properly. This can be done by cranking the engine on the starter motor with the engine disabled such that it won't start (remove coil lead or plug wires) with the hose connection loose at the gauge end of the pipe. The time to tighten the hose and cease cranking the engine is when oil spurts out! Second-hand gauges are more than likely available courtesy of a local vehicle breaker and, whether new or second-hand, make sure the gauge calibration is the unit of measure you are most familiar with.

OIL TEMPERATURE GAUGE

Having made the decision to fit an oil temperature gauge you next need to decide what type you want and where to fit the sensor. Gauges can have a wax capillary sensor or an electrical sensor; the sensor may be mounted in the sump or in a suitable oil line. If you don't have an oil cooler you may not have a suitable oil line, so bear this in mind. The gauge usually comes as part of a kit, although you may need a supplementary instrument pod to mount it in. The wax capillary type has the advantage in that you don't have to worry about electrical connections, but has the disadvantage that the capillary tubing can be broken relatively easy and, although repairable, the cost is almost equal to the price of a new unit.

TACHOMETERS

If you are after the ultimate in after market tachometers, then take a look at the range from Stack. Not only are

these highly accurate instruments, but there is a wide range of dials to suit your application. In an independent evaluation of tachometers by a car magazine the Stack rev counter was the only unit which was 100 per cent accurate. The Stack unit comes complete with extremely comprehensive fitting and usage instructions. Two switches are required, which are normally supplied with the kit. These switches control the telltale maximum display and reset telltale facility. In addition, not only can you have a tachometer telltale, but also an action replay facility of up to 5 minutes. Better still is a longer performance analysis with up to 25 minutes recall on a printout.

Stack tachometers come in two sizes, but such is the design of the larger size that it will fit the same size hole as the smaller unit (80mm) or a 116mm hole. However, the 80mm aperture required for the small unit is of smaller diameter than the usual aperture for original equipment tachometers. If this is the circumstance you find yourself in, you will need to fabricate a blanking plate to make up the difference between the old and new sizes. You can use a flat sheet of aluminium and have a hole cut in it by a local car body repair shop if you don't have the necessary tools to do the job yourself. The plate can be pop riveted in and then painted to suit. However, before fitting the plate, consider whether it might be better fitted eccentrically to the original hole in whatever position it will be easiest to see the gauge face.

The Stack tachometer has a block connector that fits into the unit at one end and to respective wires at the other end. It may be necessary to discard the old tachometer wiring and start afresh for the Stack unit. If this is the case for you, use correctly colour coded wiring

Any face calibration you like with a tell tale, a shift light function in two sizes from Stack. (Courtesy - Stack).

If you are turbocharging the engine don't forget to include a boost gauge like this one from Superchips. (Courtesy - Superchips)

from Vehicle Wiring Products Ltd or a similar supplier. Note that the Stack unit is self-illuminating and does not require the instrument light fittings used on most original or after market tachometers which can be discarded.

The Stack gauge is extremely impressive in use and a delight to watch. You should even be able to see what revs a blip on the throttle produces on a gear change.

If you cannot afford a Stack tachometer, not even a second-hand one, then shop around and buy according to what you can afford. Be advised, though, that you get what you pay for.

HEADLIGHTS
If you are doing any amount of night driving you might wish to upgrade the lighting on your car. The most obvious and easiest way to do this is by fitting some spot lights. However, since any spotlights will only work in conjunction with main beam operation you will be no better off whatsoever when driving on dipped lights. It's recommended then to upgrade the headlights by fitting higher wattage quartz halogen bulbs or Xenon bulbs, either of which will produce more light than the standard bulbs. If, however, your car is so old that its existing headlights have

incandescent (tungsten) bulbs rather than quartz halogen, the entire units will need to replaced.

If you are looking for even brighter lighting, it is possible to replace 60/55W halogen bulbs with bulbs of 100/80, 130/90, or 160/100W. In the UK such high wattage bulbs are only legal on cars first used on, or after, 1 April 1986, but check the regulations for your country. **Caution!** - Although the gain in light intensity is substantial, two problems need tackling before using such bulbs. The first is that high wattage bulbs can double the loading on switches and, to overcome this, a relay must be fitted, otherwise the switch will burn out. The second is that the standard wiring is not designed for use with high wattage bulbs, and must, therefore, be replaced with wiring rated for a higher current.

Depending on the wattage of your bulbs, you may need a relay for both the main beam and the dipped circuit. The load that can be used before the switch is liable to burn out is usually 65 watts for each lamp (130W for two). Although you may be able to get away with a bit more, you should bear in mind that replacement switch units can be very expensive. Each relay is required to be wired through a fuse to the battery main feed or through the

fusebox. To avoid a spaghetti wiring maze from the live terminal of the battery, it is recommended the relay(s) be wired through the fusebox.

To determine the rating needed for the headlamp wires, divide the bulb wattage by voltage to get an amps rating. For example, take 100 watt 12 volt bulbs: 100 divided by 12 gives 8.34 amps. The nearest cable rating (erring on oversize for safety) is 8.75 amps. Standard cabling for most car headlamps is 8amps, so from this example it can be seen that 100 watt bulbs are marginal on standard wiring. 160 watt bulbs require 13.34 amps and the nearest cable size is rated at 17.5 amps. To determine the load rating for the relay - which will be required for bulbs over 100 watts - add the amp figure for each light, i.e. for two 100 watt bulbs this will be 8.34 plus 8.34, to give a requirement of 16.68 amps.

All the wiring you are likely to require, in the correct colour codes, as well as relays and a variety of connectors, can be obtained from Vehicle Wiring Products Ltd and similar companies.

AUXILIARY LIGHTING
The two main forms of auxiliary lighting are driving lights (spotlights) and foglights. For UK vehicles

registered after 1971, driving lights can only legally be wired to work in conjunction with headlight main beam, and foglights should only work when the headlight dipped beam is on. There is also UK legislation on where the lights can be mounted. Driving lights have to be no closer together than 35cm from their outside edge, and the light centre must be no higher than 106cm. Foglights have to be no nearer than 40cm from the outermost edge of the car, and the top of the light must be no higher than 106cm. Note - the information given in this section covers the UK only - legislation in your country may be different.

BATTERY

If your car has a modified engine, you might want to fit an uprated battery to ensure that even in the coldest weather the battery has sufficient cranking power to start the engine. Also, a highly tuned road engine can require considerable cranking when restarting from hot due to heat soak of the inlet manifold and carburettor(s). An important point is that the physical size of any battery is not necessarily a guide to how powerful it is. Often, a main dealer or parts supplier can advise on a suitable upgrade and an increase of 10-20 per cent is reasonable.

ALTERNATOR

Your car should have an alternator to provide power for the car's electrical systems when it is running, and to recharge the battery after it has supplied power to start the engine. If your car has a dynamo, rather than an alternator, the best thing is to get the car converted to use an alternator. If your car has a high wattage in-car entertainment system fitted, or numerous other additional/upgraded electrical items (such as high wattage auxiliary lights), you may find that the standard alternator has insufficient output and the battery is inadequately charged. The solution is to fit an alternator with a higher output. Often, another model from the same manufacturer, perhaps one used with a larger engine, will have a suitable alternator that can be used without having to make special brackets.

STARTER MOTOR

For some modified engines and for some gearbox conversions it is necessary to fit a different or high performance starter motor. Typically, such a unit may have twice the cranking power but draw less current. One source of more powerful starter motors is Cambridge Motorsport.

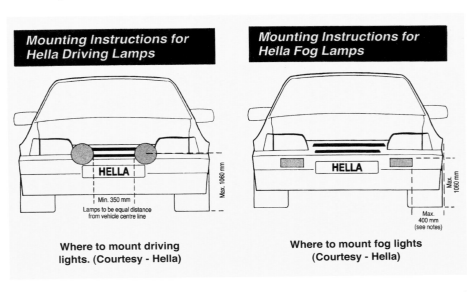

Mounting Instructions for Hella Driving Lamps

HELLA

Max. 1060 mm

Min. 350 mm
Lamps to be equal distance from vehicle centre line

Where to mount driving lights. (Courtesy - Hella)

Mounting Instructions for Hella Fog Lamps

HELLA

Max. 1060 mm

Max. 400 mm (see notes)

Where to mount fog lights (Courtesy - Hella)

When powertuning the engine don't forget the electrics, including whether the standard starter motor will cope with increased compression.

Chapter 18

Aerodynamic devices & bodywork

INTRODUCTION

Aerodynamic devices and changes to the car's bodywork will affect one, and perhaps two, aspects of performance. The fitting of an aerodynamic device should reduce drag and thereby increase straight line top speed or, in some cases, might produce downforce so that cornering speeds are increased. The problem however, is that the two desirable effects are usually mutually exclusive (though a modification which reduced air going under the car might reduce drag and reduce lift, the latter having a similar effect to increasing downforce). The reality for a fast road car is that it is all too easy to make the car go slower, and this should be borne in mind. In addition, an older car has more scope for aerodynamic improvement than a more recent model. For any modification it is first useful to consider why the bodywork is being modified in the first place.

When a car's bodywork is being modified it may be for a practical purpose (such as flaring wheelarches), aesthetic reasons (such as fitting a body kit to make the car stand out from the crowd), or some kind of aerodynamic device may be fitted (such as a wing or spoiler) in the vague hope that somehow the performance of the car will be improved. It is this latter point that we'll tackle first.

There are two basic facts about air that must be understood before considering what effect aerodynamic devices have on a car. Fact number one is that air has a weight which, though small, is measurable. Fact number two is that air, although it cannot be seen in the way that water can, is fluid. The movement of a car through air causes the air to act on the car in terms of weight, or perhaps more helpfully, in terms of pressure. Secondly, the way that the car forces its way through fluid air requires power in varying amounts.

From the first chapter of the book it is clear that a reduction in drag will increase the straightline speed of the vehicle, and improving the way the car moves through the air can raise cornering speeds. It is dangerous, and not too helpful at this point, to jump to the examples of Formula One cars, rally cars, and touring cars and decide what is good for them must be good for the road. The reason being that racing is so different from road usage. In Formula One it is often not so much straight line speed that wins races but, rather, cornering speeds. In rallying it is grip that is important in achieving high speeds on loose surfaces. In touring cars, like Formula One, it will be the cornering speed that is more important than straight line speed. The exception, from racing examples, is Le Mans where the 2 mile plus Mulsanne straight is of prime importance.

However, in all racing the aerodynamic performance can be tailored to suit the type of race, circuit, and conditions. A final point to consider is that race tracks are very smooth surfaces without the bumps, potholes and so forth found on the public highway.

The key to understanding what aerodynamic devices are useful for the road is in the relationship between drag and downforce; the less drag a vehicle has, the higher its straight line top speed will be. For cornering, the limitation on the speed attainable will be down to the amount of grip available. If pressure, or more helpfully, downforce can be applied to the tyres more grip is achieved. An aerodynamic device can produce the required pressure, but at the expense of increasing drag. In racing, the trade-off between drag and downforce is balanced to produce the best package. Drag is usually split into separate categories, namely: 'form drag', 'lift drag', 'interference drag', and 'service drag'. Form drag is the drag created by the basic shape of the car. Lift drag is created by air that passes underneath the car and creates undesirable lift. Interference drag, also known as 'skin drag', is created by mirrors, trim, etc, and the surface of the car itself. Service drag is created by the passage of air through the car for cooling and ventilation purposes. So much for the bare basics, now it's time to take a brief look at what bits can do what. You should bear in mind, however, that we are looking purely at the theory here (a poorly designed product will achieve little or nothing, and many manufacturers do not test their products in a wind tunnel to see if they work or not).

SPOILERS
Front spoiler
A decent front spoiler, or maybe a deeper front spoiler, can improve the coefficient of drag of your car. Depending on how good or bad the car is, speed improvements of 2-4mph

might be seen when a spoiler is fitted. At high cornering speeds a good front spoiler might also reduce front end lift and provide increased traction for the steered wheels and for the driven wheels of FWD cars.

Rear spoiler
A rear spoiler works by changing the way the air separates at the tail of the car and thereby reduces drag. However, unlike the front spoiler it is much easier to increase drag here than reduce it. As far as increasing downforce goes, most rear spoilers aren't going to make much difference on a road car.

Aside from fitting spoilers, it is worth looking a step further and considering a whole kit of parts that comprise some or all of the above as well as changing the styling of the car (body or styling kits).

BODYWORK KITS
A great many bodywork or styling

kits will change the overall look of the car, and ones that include properly developed spoilers may improve the overall performance of the car too. On the negative side, all bodywork kits add extra weight, and that's bad for performance. Most kits are styling, rather than performance, orientated - and you need to bear that in mind. As far as choosing a good kit instead of a bad one, you can ask if any information is available on the aerodynamic performance of various kits - but be prepared to be disappointed.

ROLL BARS & ROLL CAGES
For a soft top car (including removable hardtops) it is worth fitting roll hoops or the more motorsport orientated roll bar for safety reasons alone. If you want to fit a full roll cage to the bodyshell, either for safety or to increase torsional stiffness, the performance benefit will be in cornering where suspension geometry changes due to body flex will

A combination of body kits complete with a neat paint job can transorm your fast road car as shown here. (Courtesy - Wings West)

A well designed front air dam like the one on this radically modified VW Golf can improve the aerodynamic efficiency of the car and thereby increase top speed. (Courtesy - Wings West)

It's important to have a suitable rear wing, shown here, because the downforce it generates will increase drag. (Courtesy - Wings West)

be reduced. The downside is that a full cage is heavy and expensive. A lighter but stronger cage made from T45 tubing (or US equivalents) is lighter than cold drawn steel (CDS), but has a price penalty. Safety Devices can supply and fit, or even design, a cage

Fitted rollover bars are a must for open top cars in case it all goes wrong. (Courtesy - Safety Devices)

Rollover bars can also be chromed. (Courtesy - Safety Devices)

If your car is going to see some motorsports use then a race approved fitted roll cage will be required and need not be intrusive. The roll bar here looks to be more for styling and, while functional, may not be race approved.

for any car, and are acknowledged experts.

BONNET LOUVRES

The idea behind the bonnet louvre is to allow hot air in the engine bay to escape and they can be seen on the 1960s Jaguar E-Type and on the more modern Sierra Cosworth, both cars with stunning performance. Bonnet louvres are simply angled slots that on the Jaguar are punched into the metal and on the Sierra are in fibreglass panels. You can have the bonnet (hood) or any other panel on your car louvred.

If you want the punched metal look, then Kool Louvre can punch your bonnet for you. The main restriction on the number, size and, most importantly, position of the louvres is the frame of the bonnet itself - the framework on the underside of the panel. All that you need to do is take the bonnet to Kool Louvre, or a similar specialist, and they will do the rest. Note however, that the panel will require repainting afterwards.

If you want the fibreglass louvres in your bonnet then you will either need to do the work yourself or find a reputable body shop that will do the work for you. Once you have purchased the louvre inserts the bonnet will need to be neatly cut to allow for the insertion of the louvres. Fastening of the louvre can be by fasteners such as pop rivets or, if you prefer, fibreglass.

Louvres can be GRP inserts (left) or punched into the metal itself (right), and can aid performance by reducing under bonnet temperatures.

WHEELARCHES

If you have fitted wider wheels and tyres or altered the track of your car, or any combination of the three, you may find that the edge of the tyre protrudes past the bodywork of the car. It is a legal requirement in the UK that the tyre edge must not protrude past the wing (fender) edge and, therefore, you'll need to fit a wheelarch extension kit, modify the arch flare, or choose a full body kit that has flared arches (legislation will vary in other countries). Looking at the extension kit first, there is a wide range of wheelarch kits on the market and most of these will be of fibreglass or aluminium. Fitting may be by pop rivet or self tapping screw. Before fitting you need to consider the wheel travel and whether or not you need to cut back the standard arch before fitting the kit in order to allow for sufficient wheel travel without fouling.

An alternative to fitting an extension kit is to flare the existing arches. This can be achieved by cutting the arch rim at short intervals, peeling the arch up, and then welding the cuts back together. The arch will need to be finished with body filler to get a smooth finish. The obvious disadvantage to this method is that it can be expensive and requires the paintwork to be resprayed.

WINDOW TINTING

There are a range of reasons for having tinted windows on your vehicle: improving the looks, reducing interior glare and heat, through to increasing the privacy and security of your vehicle. Depending on your car it may be possible to purchase replacement glass that has a factory tint or you could ring around breakers yards till you find a car, or possibly cars, that have the tinted glass you need. If, however, tinted glass was never available for your car, or is no longer available anywhere, you still have the option of getting your existing windows tinted. A point to note here is that if your existing glass is deeply or even micro scratched it will not tint well.

There are two ways to have the windows tinted on your car: you can buy a kit and do it yourself, or you can have the job done professionally. Although I am a great believer in do-it-yourself solutions, this is one area where I think the job is best done by a professional. The reason for this is that window tinting is not as easy a job as it looks. If you don't believe me just look around to see how many botched, bubbly and wrinkled tinted windows there are around. However, if you are confident you can do the job then go for it.

If you are going for the professional approach then Pentagon Auto-Tint is a well respected company.

A wheelarch flaring kit will be required where wider wheels and tyres have been fitted as shown here. (Courtesy - Wings West)

When your car - like this one - looks fast even when it is stationary, you know you have a success! (Courtesy - Wings West)

Tinted windows like the smoke effect shown here from Pentago Auto-Tint are businesslike, but replacing side windows with tinted polycarbonate is the weight saving performance solution. (Courtesy - Pentagon Auto-Tint)

Chapter 19

Dynamometer tuning & road development

INTRODUCTION

Dynamometer tuning and road development will affect two aspects of performance: acceleration and straight line top speed, both by virtue of increases in engine power. However, as with any gain in power, cornering speeds may also be improved so, ultimately, three aspects of performance may be improved. Aspects of performance aside, dynamometer tuning and road development are both ways to ensure that the parts fitted to your car are not only working in harmony with each other, but are calibrated to achieve the best power output. Failing to get this right can result in expensive failures and disappointment.

DYNAMOMETER TUNING

There are two distinct types of dynamometer: the engine dyno, and the chassis dyno (sometimes known as a 'rolling road'). The engine dyno is an engine test bed where the engine is run

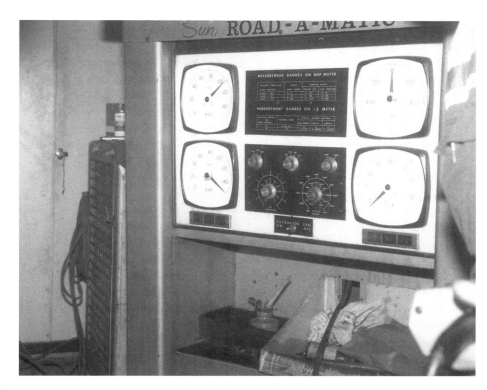

Time for half scale as the power reaches the end of the standard scale at 150bhp on the rolling road and with an engine that produced less than half this in standard tune.

independently of the car, with power readings taken direct from the flywheel. A few engine tuners will sell you an engine (or have yours rebuilt) after they have tested it on an engine dyno. Most, however, will only have used an engine dyno for development of an engine specification rather then to check the output of any subsequently built engine (or rebuild) they are selling you. If you are buying an engine off-the-shelf with a quoted power output, it's worth asking them how they came to the quoted power figure.

The chassis dyno, or rolling road, is the type of dyno you are most likely to encounter. The power readings are taken from the driven wheels of the vehicle which are run against a pair (two pairs for 4WD vehicles) of rollers set flush in a floor. There is a new type of chassis dyno which has been around in the USA for some time but is only just beginning to be seen in Europe. It is called the Dynojet (not to be confused with Dynomet tuning) and is quite different in several respects to the traditional rolling road, but broadly achieves the same result, albeit in a different way.

Because of the time taken to remove an engine from a vehicle and set it up on an engine dyno, and then put the engine back into the vehicle, the engine dyno is not something you are ever likely to use, let alone after each time you change something on the engine of your car. The remainder of this chapter will, therefore, concentrate on the chassis dyno alone.

CHASSIS DYNO
What a chassis dyno can do
A chassis dyno is the best place to learn what your engine is doing across its entire power range. A dyno session will provide information on brake horsepower and torque output, detail actual vehicle speeds, precise engine rpm and exhaust emissions across the whole operating range of the engine. Primarily, though, a dyno session is used for tuning the engine for maximum power, calibrating the fuel system and setting the ignition timing. A point to note is that the power figures produced at a chassis dyno session are for power at the driven wheels. This figure is then converted to a hypothetical figure at the flywheel, and in some cases the method used to produce the calculation is more accurate than others.

The other important fact to note about the power figures produced, is that they cannot be realistically compared to power figures for other vehicles measured on a different dyno. This is because calibration of dynos can vary, and even consistent use of the same dyno can produce variations in power figures due to atmospheric changes and so on. Therefore, the dyno is not a means of obtaining power figures to be boasted about (even less so lied about), but should be regarded more as an instrument to get the best results from your vehicle's engine on the day you carry out a dyno run, in order for the engine to be running at its maximum efficiency.

Choosing a chassis dyno
There are numerous chassis dynos and operators and so, on the face of it, the obvious choice would be to book a session at the geographically nearest. However, the nearest might not be the best, or the best for you. Although dyno operators see diverse vehicles on their dynos, some tend to specialise in one particular make of car or engine. Some may not be as competent as others and destroy more than the occasional engine under dubious circumstances. If your vehicle is 4WD you will have a more

More expensive to use than the chassis dyno or rolling road is the flywheel dyno shown here with a Peugeot engine being mounted.

limited choice of dynos because not all have the two sets of rollers required. If your car's engine has a Superchip, then you might prefer to find a dyno operator with the Superchip modem facility. Superchips aside, some dyno installations are more modern than others and produce a printout of the vehicle's performance. What really counts, however, is the ability of the dyno operator. In summary, choose carefully and ask around to get at least one good personal recommendation.

Preparing for the session

Before you go to the dyno session you first need to book an appointment. Next, make sure that the engine is in good running order. Get the car serviced, or do it yourself, in regard to changing sparkplugs, oil and filter, ignition points (where fitted), and the air filter. Note that as far as setting up the ignition system and fuelling calibrations, that is for the dyno operator to sort. That said, it is useful if you know what the basic settings are, even after fitting modified parts, and, where possible, to know the sizes of carburettor jets and needles (where applicable). Lastly take a pen and paper and a friend to record information about the session, such as oil pressure, running temperatures, and so on.

What happens at a typical chassis dyno session

Having turned up for the appointment, the most important thing is to have a chat to the dyno operator about the specification of the engine, and to discuss any problems you know the engine has, such as flat spots or hesitation at any point in the rev range. In turn be prepared for the operator to ask you questions about the sort of use the car is put to. Having finished talking, it is time for action and, depending on the operator, you

may be asked to drive the vehicle on the rollers or generally keep out of the way.

The vehicle will be driven onto the rollers such that the driven wheels are in contact with the rollers. The undriven wheels will be chocked and the vehicle strapped down using some tie downs. An emission analyser will be connected to the exhaust system and an electronic diagnostic system will be connected to the vehicle's ignition system. The engine will be started and the operator's ignition diagnostic will quickly show up any basic ignition problems, such as a bad leads or an arcing distributor cap. If any faults are found at this point they will need rectification before any further progress can be made. At this point a visual check for oil and water leaks might be made, as well as checks for any other obvious problems.

Next the first rolling run will be undertaken. On this run the objective of the dyno operator is to establish a good ignition setting. The operator will do this by 'swinging' the distributor (having loosened the fastening first) while the vehicle is being driven on the rollers at an engine rpm that corresponds to the maximum advance the distributor produces, usually at about the mid range power point of the engine. Once this has been done the first run is finished. Once the rollers are stationary the dyno operator will tighten up the distributor clamp and, using whatever ignition diagnostic he has wired up, either an oscilloscope or strobe (perhaps both) tell you what the static ignition timing figure is. This setting will be unique to your vehicle's engine and tuning setup. If you are really serious about ignition timing, it's possible to plot optimum readings right through the rev range. This information can then be used to adjust the distributor's ignition curve to the

ideal for the engine. However, if your vehicle has a fully electronic system that doesn't even have a distributor there is probably not a lot that can be done at this point (unless the car is fitted with a Superchip), other than to note how well the management chip is performing. If the car is fitted with a Superchip and the dyno operator is a Superchip modem dealer then it is possible for a whole host of variables to be modified by downloading data, direct from Superchips' main computer.

Following on from the first engine run, the next run is carried out to establish how well the engine is performing throughout the rev range. The operator will be watching the CO reading of the exhaust gas analysis to see if the air/fuel mixture is too rich or too weak at any point in the rev range. If the mixture is so weak that there is a risk of the pistons being damaged, even holed, the run will be terminated and the problem rectified before the run is recommenced. After this run is completed the operator will need to know the use the vehicle is put to in order to set the mixture accordingly. For instance, a full race mixture is richer than a road use only mixture, though the final say is yours, guided, of course, by the advice the dyno operator gives you.

Once the mixture settings have been agreed upon, and in the case of a carburated engine, jets and needles changed, a full power run can be undertaken. However, as with ignition settings, if your vehicle has the fuelling controlled wholly by a management chip, there is probably not a lot of action that can be taken other than noting how well the chip has performed (unless you have a Superchip, in which case it can be modified).

The full power run is pretty

awesome whichever way you look at it. Some people cringe and hope for the best as the vehicle is driven at full power on the rollers, others sit back relaxed and grin from ear to ear. Whatever your attitude to the full power run, it is the one that really matters. Depending on the sophistication of the dyno, a printout of the entire power output plotted against the engine rpm may be produced. If one isn't, it is time to put your friend to good use and let him/her note each power figure at 500rpm increments, the figures can then be plotted on graph paper at leisure after the dyno session. During the full power run, more so than the previous runs, a close eye needs to be kept on engine coolant temperature, oil temperature (if you have a gauge), and, not least, oil pressure. If any of these give cause for concern at any time during the proceedings the engine should be switched off immediately. If you are the person driving the car on the rollers, then this is your responsibility. Note that, despite the presence of a large cooling fan in the dyno bay, most vehicles will run slightly on the hot side. If the dyno run does highlight a problem in this area, guidance on how to resolve the problem is given in the relevant chapters of this book.

When the dyno session has been completed, and there may have been more than one full power run depending on how things went, the operator may ask you to take the vehicle for a short drive on the highway. This is an interesting and revealing moment, because you will feel the benefit of the dyno tune both in the smoothness of the power delivery and in the increased power liberated by the dyno calibration changes.

The bill for the use of the dyno session is usually based on an hourly rate, plus the cost of any parts, such as

The G Tech performance meter - stick it on your car windscreen and plug it into the cigarette lighter socket.

plug leads, carb jets, etc. Although the bottom line on the bill may be quite high, and this is what puts people off dyno sessions, it is a modest cost given the gains in engine power achieved and the data gathered. If the dyno session has highlighted an engine problem, and the session has had to be prematurely terminated, you have at least saved yourself an expensive engine failure.

The first dyno session should most definitely not be seen as the last or only session required. As further developments and modifications of the engine are undertaken further visits to the dyno should be made. Where finances prohibit this for any length of time, a sad fact of life, keep a record of the work done and the effects produced for future reference.

Finally, the dyno session should be the 'icing on the cake' of your tuning project, so enjoy it.

ROAD DEVELOPMENT

It is difficult to do much road development in respect of power tuning the engine unless you have access to a private road, test or race track or airfield. Either way, one essential tool is the G Tech performance meter. The meter will carry out various measurements, including horsepower measurement, and various acceleration times and G-force measurements. It can be used to find out what effect changes to gearing and traction have on acceleration times, as well as comparing how much grip one tyre has compared to another (by reference to lateral G). It is relatively simple to use, and though fairly expensive, not prohibitively so. It is a useful instrument but no substitute for dyno testing, rather a supplement to it.

Chapter 20
Tools, fasteners & plumbing

TOOLS

If you intend to carry out any of the modifications and work detailed in this book, you'll need a reasonable set of tools to work with. If you are spending most of your available money on bits for your car, there will not be a lot left over for tool purchases. However, the right tools can save you frustration, and quite often money too, by enabling you to do some of the more difficult jobs yourself. Only purchase good quality tools, such as Snap-on, that have a lifetime guarantee as they always work out cheaper in the long run. If your pocket doesn't run to buying sets of expensive tools, still try to purchase good quality items when you know they will get a lot of use. Remember as well that good quality second-hand tools can be a money saver.

Depending on the make, model, and age of your car, you may find the fastenings are metric or imperial AF. The latter is more common on older British cars, but you will still find that many modified parts will be metric anyway and you will need to adjust your tool purchasing to suit. Although it is nice to buy spanners and screwdrivers in sets, it's worth purchasing a single spanner, screwdriver, or socket for a particular job or fastener.

Many car accessory shops will hire you more expensive items such as hub pullers. Always hire a hydraulic engine crane for engine removal rather than use a cheap hoist. The cheaper hoists are slow to use and not worth the expense of outright purchase compared to occasional crane hire.

Here is a list of tools I recommend you have. It is by no means exhaustive, but most, if not all, these tools will be required at one time or another:

Set of AF or metric combination spanners (wrenches)
Set of AF or metric ring spanners (wrenches)
Set of AF or metric open-ended spanners (wrenches)
Sparkplug spanner (wrench)
Brake adjuster tool (check type before purchase)
Sump plug tool
Set of Allen (hex drive) keys
Set of feeler gauges (metric or Imperial as required)
Wire brush
Set of plain head screwdrivers
Set of crosshead (Philips) screwdrivers
Set of posidrive screwdrivers (not to be confused with Philips type)
Hacksaw
Pliers
Combination pliers
Grease gun (if applicable)
Torque wrench
Half inch drive socket (wrench) set AF or metric - largest set you can afford
Mole grips
Impact driver
Set of cold chisels
Dot punch

Pop riveter (riveting pliers)
Axle stands (jack stands)
Trolley jack
Ball joint splitter (screw thread type)
Crimping pliers (strippers/cutters)
Soldering iron
Circuit tester (12V)
Heavy hammer
Oil filter wrench or socket
Stilsons (pipe wrench)
Electric drill
Strobe light or timing light and
diagnostic
Jemmy (crow bar/wrecking bar)
Medium flat file
Small flat file
Round file
Easy out extractors (for broken studs)
Electrical extension lead
Decent tool box to keep everything in

WORKING ON YOUR CAR AND USE OF TOOLS

Warning! - The most important consideration when working on your car is your safety. Most workshop manuals will give a list of do's and don'ts, so I won't repeat them. What I will offer is a few tips that should come in useful, save some bother and, perhaps, money too.

If you come across any stubborn and seized (frozen) fasteners, applying heat to the fastener with a blowlamp or welding torch is usually much more effective than the use of penetrating oil. If you have neither of these but can get the component to the household kitchen, stick it in the stove! Also, be sure to have a suitable replacement fastener before proceeding to destroy the old one. Another solution for stubborn fasteners is to consider Snap-on's patented open ended wrench/spanner with gripping teeth which gives you more turning power and strength than any other design of open end spanner, it is called 'Flank Drive Plus', not to be confused with the

company's normal flank drive system. Force is directed away from the weaker corners of the fastener and directed to the stronger flats. For stubborn fasteners this will make a genuine difference.

If you are using a tool in a difficult area where, if you drop it, retrieval is likely to be difficult if not impossible, tie a length of string onto the tool with the other end fastened around your wrist.

Finally, when working on

components, use a workbench and vice if possible, although many jobs can be done by improvising. A word of caution, improvisation does not mean taking a risk with your personal safety. If you need expert assistance, a local garage will often help for no charge at all, or a beer at the local pub.

FASTENERS

Having a decent tool kit is only half way to doing the job properly.

Snap-on Flank Drive Plus spanner starts to round off the head of the test piece at a reading of just over 80 - proof that extra turning torque can be achieved before the head rounds off.

Typical average spanner starts to round off the head of the test piece at a reading of just over 50.

Torque test rig from Snap-on, reading shows what can be achieved with one of their Flank Drive Plus spanners – the 'tell-tale' reading at 80.

Whenever taking components apart and fitting modified parts, use new set screws, bolts and nuts. Most of the set screws, bolts and nuts you will be working with will either be imperial UNF thread (Unified Normal Fine) or Metric. In the absence of a suitable test gauge or other measuring equipment, a general guide to establishing whether a set screw or bolt is imperial or metric will be to look at the markings on the head. A letter S or sometimes T will generally be indicative that the fastener is imperial, while numbers such as 8.8 are indicative that it is a metric fastener. Note that engine and transmission fasteners tend to deviate from these markings and generally are of a much higher strength. Also, keep an eye out for UNC (Unified Normal Course) and coarse metric fasteners which are often used with aluminium components and are stronger than the thread they are tightened into. In other words, unlike normal bolts, the thread will strip out of the component before the bolt shears. Stainless steel fasteners are much less strong than plated steel, and have a tensile strength of 45.3 ton ft/in sq and yield stress of 29.1 ton ft/in sq. When using Nylock nuts, or similar, remember they should only be re-used if the nylon insert at the end of the nut is in reasonable condition. Lubricate fasteners with Copperslip, or similar, unless there are special reasons for not doing so.

Conventional fasteners are available from Mr Fast'ner Ltd and others. The strongest fasteners and studs that you can get are the ARP range from the USA, and are ideal for cylinder heads, clutches, flywheels, con-rods, and other critical applications. They are widely available in the USA and through several specialist parts suppliers in the UK, including Kent Cams.

For any application where weight is at a premium, and the component is in an unstressed area, you could use a special lightweight fastener. One such choice would be the aerospace grade aluminium bolt, screw, and nut range from AWF. These fastenings are 60 per cent lighter than steel and have a tensile strength of 35 tons. An alternative from AWF are fasteners in BT16 titanium which is 45 per

Stainless steel fasteners for less demanding situations ease the problem of corrosion.

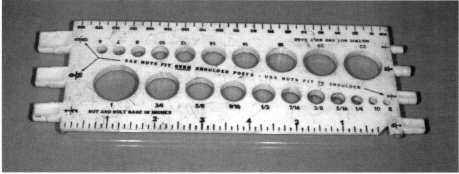

A nut and bolt sizing gauge like the one shown here is a valuable aid to establishing fastener sizes.

Don't forget to use high quality fastenings in critical areas, such as these by ARP. They are cheaper than an engine failure caused by a fastener failing.

Alloy and titanium fasteners in a multitude of colours from AWF are one way to save weight. (Courtesy - AWF Ltd)

cent lighter than steel. This particular grade of titanium is more elastic than other grades and will bend before it snaps which can be handy. Note that whichever lightweight material you use, care must be taken that the component is in an unstressed area. A good use for lightweight fastenings would be the retention of the window winder mechanism, possibly the door catch striker plate. But a bad use would be to fasten the door hinges to the car.

PLUMBING

When you look through the Goodridge catalogue for the first time you may be daunted by the unusual terminology used. BGC Motorsport Components prints a simple guide to the Goodridge system which it kindly agreed to me borrowing from for this section.

The Goodridge system is based on UNF (same as JIC) hose ends which are compatible with most things you will find on older British cars. Unfortunately, the most likely exceptions will be just those parts you intend to plumb, such as fuel and oil lines, which may use metric, BSP, or NPTF threads. The recommended solution to such incompatibility is to use an adapter with UNF fittings at each end of the line.

To work out what size bore hose you require you will need to understand the dash size. The dash size is used to associate a hose size to a thread fitting and is given in the above table.

SUMMARY

Although decent tools and quality fasteners may seem like a luxury, they are money well spent and not worth skimping on. Not least, they can turn a nightmare into a pleasure.

BRAIDED HOSE AND THREAD STYLES

DASH SIZE	JIC THREAD	BSP THREAD	NPTF THREAD
-3	$\frac{3}{8} \times 24$	$\frac{1}{8} \times 28$	$\frac{1}{8} \times 27$
-4	$\frac{7}{16} \times 20$	$\frac{1}{4} \times 18$	$\frac{1}{4} \times 18$
-5	$\frac{1}{2} \times 20$	-	-
-6	$\frac{9}{16} \times 18$	$\frac{3}{8} \times 19$	$\frac{3}{8} \times 18$
-7	$\frac{5}{8} \times 18$	-	-
-8	$\frac{3}{4} \times 16$	$\frac{1}{2} \times 14$	
-10	$\frac{7}{8} \times 14$	$\frac{5}{8} \times 14$	-
-12	$1\frac{1}{16} \times 12$	$\frac{3}{4} \times 14$	$\frac{3}{4} \times 14$

Suppliers

AP Racing
Wheler Road
Seven Stars Industrial Estate
Coventry
Warwickshire CV3 4LB
Tel: 01203 639595
www.apracing.com

AWF
Gratton House
Gratton Street
Cheltenham
Gloucestershire GL50 2AS
Tel: 01242 228111

B&M Racing & Performance Products
9142 Independence Avenue
Chatsworth
CA 91311
United States of America.
Tel: 818 882 6422
www.bmracing.com

Burlen Fuel Systems
Spitfire House
Castle Road
Salisbury
Wiltshire SP1 3SA
Tel: 01722 412500
www.burlen.co.uk

Burton Power
617-631 Eastern Avenue

Ilford
Essex IG2 6PN
Tel: 020 8554 2281
www.burtonpower.com

Cambridge Motorsport
Great Gransden
Nr Sandy
Bedfordshire SG19 3AH
Tel: 01767 677969
www.cambridgemotorsport.com

Digi Dash
8 Woodcroft
Woodside
Telford
Shropshire TF7 5ND
Tel: 01952 582051

Edelbrock
2700 California Street
Torrance
CA 90503
United States of America
Tel: 310 781 2222
www.edelbrock.com

Fibresports
34-36 Bowlers Croft
Cranes Industrial Estate
Basildon
Essex SS14 3ED
Tel: 01268 527331

Flyin' Miata
331 South 13th St
Grand Junction
CO
81501
United States of America
Tel: 800 359 6957
www.flyinmiata.com

Fluidyne – www.fluidyne.com
Available from a range of dealers listed on
their website

Focussport
1350 North Hundley Street
Anaheim
CA
92806
United States of America
Tel: 714 630 6353
www.focussport.com

Fuel System Enterprises
180 Hersham Road
Hersham
Walton on thames
Surrey KT12 5QE
Tel: 01932 231973
www.fuelsystem.co.uk

Goodridge (UK) Ltd
Exeter Airport
Exeter

Devon EX5 2UP
Tel: 01392 369090

Guy Croft Racing Engines
Unit 3B
Whisby Road
Lincoln
Lincolnshire LN6 3QT
Tel: 01522 705 222
www.guy-croft.com

HKS - www.hksusa.com
Available from a range of dealers listed on
their website

Holbay Consolidations Ltd
Grundisburgh
Woodbridge
Suffolk IP13 6TJ
Tel: 01473 738738
www.holbay.co.uk

Kool Louvres
14 Walton Way
Aylesbury
Buckinghamshire HP21 7JL
Tel: 01296 88548

Procharger Accessible Technologies Inc
14801 W
114th Terrace
Lenexa
KS 66215
United States of America
Tel: 913 338 2886
www.procharger.com

Quaife Power Systems
Vestry Road
Otford
Sevenoaks
Kent TN14 5EL
Tel: 01732 741144
www.quaife.co.uk

Rally Design
Units 9 & 10
North Quay
Upper Brents Industrial Estate

Faversham
Kent ME13 7DZ,
Tel: 01795 531871

Reco-Prop (UK) Ltd
Unit 4
Newtown Trading Estate
Chase Street
Luton
Bedfordshire LU1 3QZ
Tel: 01582 412110

Safety Devices Ltd
Regal Drive
Soham
Cambridge
Cambridgeshhire CB7 5BE
Tel: 01353 724200
www.safetydevices.co.uk

Serck Services Motorsport
Unit 9-11
Bullsbrook Road
Brook Industrial Estate
Hayes
Middlesex UB4 0JZ
Tel: 020 8813 7470
www.serckservicesmotorsport.co.uk/

Speedograph Richfield
Rolleston Drive
Arnold
Nottingham NG5 7JR
Tel: 0115 926 4235
www.speedograph-richfield.com

Steering Developments Ltd
Unit 5
Eastman Way
Hemel Hempstead
Hertfordshire HP2 7HF
Tel: 01422 212918

Superchips Ltd
Buckingham Industrial Park
Buckingham MK18 1XJ
Tel: 01280 816781
www.superchips.co.uk

Think Automotive Ltd
292 Worton Road
Isleworth
Middlesex TW7 6EL
Tel: 0208 568 1172

TWM Induction
325D Rutherford St
Goleta
CA 93117
United States of America.
Tel: 805 967 9478
www.twminduction.com

Unorthodox Racing Inc
11 Brandywine Dr.
Deer Park
NY 11729
United States of America
Tel: 631 586 9525
www.unorthodoxracing.com

Vegantune Limited
17 Gruneisen Road
Finchley
London N3 1LS
Tel: 0208 343 0618

Vibra - Technics Automotive Ltd
90 Cavendish Road
Knighton fields
Leicester
Leicestershire LE2 7PH
Tel: 0116 2835052
www.vibratechnics.freeserve.co.uk

Whiteline Automotive
4 Lincoln St
Minto NSW 2566
Australia
Tel: 61 2 9603 0111
www.whiteline.com.au

www.wingswestinternational.com -
worldwide addresses from their web pages.

*Note: Products from other companies are
available through a range of reputable
retail tuning outlets.*

Veloce *SpeedPro* books -

ISBN 1 903706 76 9   ISBN1 903706 91 2   ISBN 1 903706 77 7   ISBN 1 903706 78 5   ISBN 1 901295 73 7   ISBN 1 903706 75 0

ISBN 1 901295 62 1   ISBN 1 874105 70 7   ISBN 1 903706 60 2   ISBN 1 903706 92 0   ISBN 1 903706 94 7   ISBN 1 901295 26 5

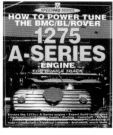 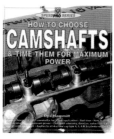 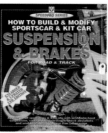   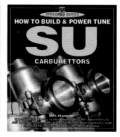

ISBN 1 901295 07 9   ISBN 1 903706 59 9   ISBN 1 903706 73 4   ISBN 1 904788 78-5   ISBN 1 901295 76 1   ISBN 1 903706 98 X

  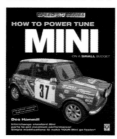  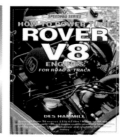 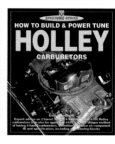

ISBN 1 903706 99 8   ISBN 1 901295 63 X   ISBN 1-904788-84-X   ISBN 1-904788-22-X   ISBN 1 903706 17 3   ISBN 1 903706 61 0

 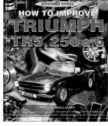 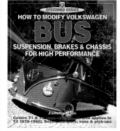 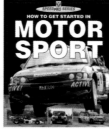  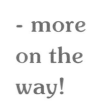

- more
on the
way!

ISBN 1 903706 80 7   ISBN 1 903706 68 8   ISBN 1 903706 14 9   ISBN 1 903706 70 X   ISBN 1 903706 72 6

Index